D1046147

KEEPING THE U.S. COMPUTER AND COMMUNICATIONS INDUSTRY COMPETITIVE: CONVERGENCE OF COMPUTING, COMMUNICATIONS, AND ENTERTAINMENT

A COLLOQUIUM REPORT BY THE

COMPUTER SCIENCE AND TELECOMMUNICATIONS BOARD

COMMISSION ON PHYSICAL SCIENCES, MATHEMATICS, AND APPLICATIONS

NATIONAL RESEARCH COUNCIL

NATIONAL ACADEMY PRESS
WASHINGTON, D.C. 1995

NOTICE: The project that is the subject of this report was approved by the Governing Board of the National Research Council, whose members are drawn from the councils of the National Academy of Sciences, the National Academy of Engineering, and the Institute of Medicine. The members of the committee responsible for the report were chosen for their special competences and with regard for appropriate balance.

This report has been reviewed by a group other than the authors according to procedures approved by a Report Review Committee consisting of members of the National Academy of Sciences, the National Academy of Engineering, and the Institute of Medicine.

Support for this project was provided by the following organizations: Air Force Office of Scientific Research (under Contract N00014-87-J-1110), Advanced Research Projects Agency (under Contract N00014-87-J-1110), Apple Computer Corporation, Department of Energy (under Grant DE-FG05-87ER25029), Digital Equipment Corporation, Intel Corporation, International Business Machines Corporation, National Aeronautics and Space Administration (under Grant CDA-9119792), National Science Foundation (under Grant CDA-9119792), and Office of Naval Research (under Contract N00014-87-J-1110). Any opinions, findings, conclusions, or recommendations expressed in this material are those of the authors and do not necessarily reflect the views of the sponsors.

Library of Congress Catalog Card Number 94-66573
International Standard Book Number 0-309-05089-8

Additional copies of this report are available from:

National Academy Press
2101 Constitution Avenue, N.W.
Box 285
Washington, DC 20055
800-624-6242
202-334-3313 (in the Washington Metropolitan Area)

B-455

This report is also available on the National Academy of Sciences' Internet host. It may be accessed via World Wide Web at http://www.nas.edu.

Printed in the United States of America

STEERING COMMITTEE ON KEEPING THE U.S. COMPUTER AND COMMUNICATIONS INDUSTRY COMPETITIVE: CONVERGENCE OF COMPUTING, COMMUNICATIONS, AND ENTERTAINMENT

The National Academy of Sciences is a private, nonprofit, self-perpetuating society of distinguished scholars engaged in scientific and engineering research, dedicated to the furtherance of science and technology and to their use for the general welfare. Upon the authority of the charter granted to it by Congress in 1863, the Academy has a mandate that requires it to advise the federal government on scientific and technical matters. Dr. Bruce Alberts is president of the National Academy of Sciences.

The National Academy of Engineering was established in 1964, under the charter of the National Academy of Sciences, as a parallel organization of outstanding engineers. It is autonomous in its administration and in the selection of its members, sharing with the National Academy of Sciences the responsibility for advising the federal government. The National Academy of Engineering also sponsors engineering programs aimed at meeting national needs, encourages education and research, and recognizes the superior achievements of engineers. Dr. Robert M. White is president of the National Academy of Engineering.

The Institute of Medicine was established in 1970 by the National Academy of Sciences to secure the services of eminent members of appropriate professions in the examination of policy matters pertaining to the health of the public. The Institute acts under the responsibility given to the National Academy of Sciences by its congressional charter to be an adviser to the federal government and, upon its own initiative, to identify issues of medical care, research, and education. Dr. Kenneth I. Shine is president of the Institute of Medicine.

The National Research Council was organized by the National Academy of Sciences in 1916 to associate the broad community of science and technology with the Academy's purposes of furthering knowledge and advising the federal government. Functioning in accordance with general policies determined by the Academy, the Council has become the principal operating agency of both the National Academy of Sciences and the National Academy of Engineering in providing services to the government, the public, and the scientific and engineering communities. The Council is administered jointly by both Academies and the Institute of Medicine. Dr. Bruce Alberts and Dr. Robert M. White are chairman and vice chairman, respectively, of the National Research Council.

Preface

This report on digital convergence is the third in a series of Computer Science and Telecommunications Board (CSTB) reports focusing on the competitive status of the U.S. computer industry. The first series report, *Keeping the U.S. Computer Industry Competitive: Defining the Agenda* (National Academy Press, Washington, D.C., 1990), provided insights from leaders of computer-related businesses and research programs on the broad industry complex and its various segments. The second series report, *Keeping the U.S. Computer Industry Competitive: Systems Integration* (National Academy Press, Washington, D.C., 1992), presented expert examination of a technology and business arena in which the United States has shown leadership, systems integration, to further understanding of how to maintain if not extend that strong performance. This third report builds on a theme in the first two, the close coupling of computing and communications in the development of new technologies, goods, and services. It explores the broader integration of information processing, communication, and generation that is reflected in the convergence of computing, communications, and entertainment. It reinforces the importance of communications that has been evident in each report by broadening the series title to *Keeping the U.S. Computer and Communications Industry Competitive*. In addition to discussing conditions, opportunities, and risks for competitiveness, it also addresses implications of the subject technologies and their uses for the daily lives of citizens.

Digital convergence is the most volatile topic considered in CSTB's competitiveness series. From the time CSTB selected the topic, through the time it held a colloquium on it, to this time of publication, several waves of interest and opinion have coursed through the news media and, by extension, the business community and popular attention. As project special advisor and industry executive Robert W. Lucky observed, there has been a "hype cycle." Opinions of where digital convergence is heading and when and how it will get there have varied over that cycle. Although this is hardly a time of stability, enough has happened to allow for greater reflection and more sober assessment of prospects than at earlier times in the past two years. Toward that end, this report is directed to decision makers in government, industry, and academia. Because so much of its subject matter is new, time-sensitive, and lacking in scholarly consideration, this report has drawn to an unusual degree on items reported in the news media. News articles are cited in part to document the hype cycle that, as noted by Lucky, itself has fed the very activity that was being reported.

In keeping with the previous volumes in this series, this report draws directly on statements made by principals from industry and academia (Appendix A) that were aired at an invitational colloquium (Appendix B). That stock of statements was updated and enlarged in this instance by a series of interviews (Appendix C) conducted by Virginia Quesada of VQ Productions Inc. The interviews were developed to support a CSTB experiment, the production of a video for limited distribution to the federal policymaking community as a companion to this report. As a few colloquium participants noted, it is out of keeping with digital convergence for CSTB to publish only in text form. The concept for the video and its initial framing were championed by steering committee member Alexander Singer, an independent film director.

Keeping the U.S. Computer and Communications Industry Competitive: Convergence of Computing, Communications, and Entertainment benefited particularly from the advice and support of special advisors to the steering committee, Samuel Fuller, Robert Lucky, and Irving Wladawsky-Berger, each of whom had contributed to the first two reports of this competitiveness series. Early drafting and organization, background consultations, and data gathering were conducted by Laura Ost, an independent science writer retained as a CSTB consultant. As always, the anonymous reviewers provided criticisms and suggestions that helped to refine and extend the discussion.

Comments on this report and suggestions of topics for future activities in this series are welcome via Internet to CSTB@nas.edu or fax to 202/334-2318.

Contents

KEEPING THE U.S. COMPUTER AND COMMUNICATIONS INDUSTRY COMPETITIVE: CONVERGENCE OF COMPUTING, COMMUNICATIONS, AND ENTERTAINMENT

1

Overview

Digital convergence—combining computing, communications, and entertainment—is taking shape in the form of new kinds of business and consumer products (goods and services) and new business ventures and alliances. It has become a regular topic in the business, trade, and mass media, yet it remains hard to define and hard to interpret in terms of its ultimate technical, business, and societal ramifications. The very term "convergence" is itself a source of confusion and ambiguity; see Box 1.1. As Samuel Ginn, former chairman and chief executive officer of Pacific Telesis Group, observed at the colloquium that served as a basis for this report,

> The whole term "convergence" continues to take on new meanings. Originally, we thought it was the combination of media and telecommunications. Then we discovered that set[-top] devices were a key part of that convergence, and then we understood that storage technology was important, and indeed, semiconductor manufacturing, and then the whole applications arena and the programming arena. Now, we understand that games and transactions and retail firms are all a part of this convergence. So this whole idea continues to evolve.

As a result, the true nature of digital convergence may not be reflected accurately by either its advocates or the popular media. Illustrating the swings in opinion, sample headlines and news story themes between mid-1993 and mid-1994 included "Multimedia Is Growing by Leaps and Bounds"; "Race for Multimedia Crown Speeding Up: Companies Team to Get Jump on Interactive Services"; "Merger to Create a Media Giant"; "With Merger's Failure, an Industry Seeks a Leader"; and "Hurdles Slow Information 'Superhypeway.'"

Box 1.1 Meaning of Convergence

We have been applying the term "convergence" to the major information, electronics, and communications industries with increasing fervor for over three decades, going back to the work and ideas coming out of Harvard University, the Massachusetts Institute of Technology, and other places in the 1960s. It is time to deal more gingerly with the term. What do we really mean by convergence? What is it shorthand for? A flurry of mergers and alliances? The common use of bits? Or is there something more fundamental to it than that? Jacob Bronowski warned of the classical error of regarding a scientific law as only shorthand for its instances. His caveat may apply here.

In mathematics, convergence is the property or process of approaching a limiting value. That meaning of the term appears the exact opposite of the wildfire of innovation expected from the convergence of industries dealt with in this report.

In physiology, convergence refers to a coordinated turning of the eyes inward to focus on an object at close range. Once again, we are confronted with a meaning that is antithetic to the far-reaching and long-range changes in thinking and behavior that we all expect.

In biology, convergence refers to the adaptive evolution of superficially similar structures in unrelated species exposed to similar environments. This meaning may be closer to what digital convergence may entail.

More superficially, convergence may simply mean a meeting ground, or a process of coming together, for example, a place where two rivers join.

SOURCE: Adapted from Martin Greenberger, University of California at Los Angeles, personal communication, July 30, 1994.

Underlying digital convergence are advances in computer hardware, telecommunications systems, and software. The unifying element is digital technology, which reduces all information to a binary code of 1s and 0s. Whereas computers and software have been digital for decades, audio and video technologies have only recently begun to go digital. Once information has a digital representation, different forms can be blended together (although digitization is not sufficient for such integration, which depends on the structures imposed on the bits) and, eventually, transmitted by wire, fiber, or wireless means. Thus, digitized material can be defined by what it does rather than the medium on which it is transported, stored, or used. Moreover, digital devices can be programmed, something that allows them to be more than passive receivers of information. A current realization of digital convergence is associated with "interactive multimedia" products; see Box 1.2.

Digital convergence could build on, blend, and redirect the functions, products, and cultures of many existing industries. Although sales figures for existing industries are neither directly comparable nor additive, they give an indication of the potential economic impact: catalogue shopping ($70 billion in current annual U.S. revenues; *WWD*, 1994),[1] broadcast advertising (currently $27 billion; Turner,

Box 1.2 Defining Interactive Multimedia

"Multimedia" usually refers to a blend of various forms of media (text, graphics, sound, video) in a digital format, but the meaning of the term varies. Multimedia computing, for example, often combines numerical data, graphics, animation, and audio, or some subset of these elements. Multimedia as a term has also been used to include interactive television and related services, such as video on demand, remote learning, home shopping, and teleconferencing. It may involve generation of content from existing basic material (as in the generation of video games using movie images and story lines, a movie aftermarket) as well as new content; the emphasis is on the composition of the media and their interaction with the content.

"Interactive" products are sometimes treated as a subset of multimedia. Whether so categorized or addressed separately, interactivity is regarded by some analysts as the pivotal feature of the new technologies.

Interactive technologies emphasize the active involvement of the user, as opposed to more passive reception of content, as via conventional broadcast media. Interactive technologies range from remote control devices (e.g., for television operation) at the low end to, at the high end, virtual reality, which may involve visual and perhaps tactile and auditory immersion in a three-dimensional computer-generated "artificial world" permitting multiuser actions and interactions. Interactivity has been gaining attention because of evidence that it can enhance education and training, on the one hand, and because it is stimulating growth of such leisure activities as games, on the other. Thus, the Internet is often offered by those familiar with it as a model for interactive communication and as a laboratory for interactive applications of digital convergence, from "newsgroups" and information-access services to multiplayer games. It is already moving to support two-way digital services with high-quality sound, animated visuals, and other elements, themselves the ingredients for products being developed or piloted by cable system operators, telephone companies, information service providers, hardware and software vendors, and other companies.

Robert Stein, a founder of the Voyager Company, said he never uses the "M word" because the combination of multiple media per se is already available on television and in movies. "I'm much more interested in the interaction, the relationship between the reader and the material, and the author and the reader, than I am in just the simple aggregate," Stein said. "Eventually, we're going to go past the aggregate. We're actually going to invent something new, although I think that is still decades away."

1993a), home video (currently $12 billion; Turner, 1993a), information services (currently $9 billion; Turner, 1993a), video games (currently $6.5 billion; Tetzeli, 1993; Pereira, 1994), consumer electronics, including TVs, VCRs, audio equipment, blank tapes, and accessories (currently $40 billion to $55 billion; Sims, 1994), and recorded music (currently $10 billion; Newman, 1994). Unknown are the new markets that digital convergence may spawn. The commercialization of the Internet and the growth of on-line services illustrate some of the possibilities. However, near-term markets tend to be overestimated or at least misestimated:

estimates of the near-term market for interactive media (e.g., CD-ROM applications) range widely from $4 billion to $14 billion annually by 1995. Projecting the fate of new markets is notoriously hard, given their small origins and uncertain prospects.[2]

A key indicator is the experience of on-line services (internal and inter-enterprise) in the business domain: computerized reservation services for airlines, legal and financial database services, 800-number help-lines, 900-number services, and others have become profitable. These services may use a somewhat different mix of media (e.g., they place a heavy emphasis on telephones), but they appear to offer an analogous experience base. A note of caution comes from the rocky experience of on-line services aimed at households; despite growth and new entries, such services have had difficulty arriving at user interfaces, pricing schemes, and product and service packages that would generate consistent profits.[3]

Computer-based services aimed at the mass market generally may become more successful, given astute marketing and management decisions as well as the expanding base in household equipment: about 95 percent of U.S. households have telephones; most households have television sets, and industry analysts estimate that up to 40 percent of all households will have interactive television in the next decade (Schwarz, 1993); over 30 million have personal computers today, and over 10 million of those have CD-ROM drives.[4] Anecdotal evidence suggests that the latter part of 1994 saw a surge in computer systems for the home, attesting both to greater interest in digital convergence products and to an expansion of the customer base from the technically sophisticated to more neophytes (Markoff, 1995b). This upgrading of home equipment could constitute a turning point for educational products, suggested Nancy Stover of YourChoice TV in a late-1994 interview. Shortages of capital in schools and homes have constrained the educational technology market for decades, but now there is a greater prospect of teachers and students having access from their homes to technology and content. Cautioned Stephen Case of America Online in another late-1994 interview, "Despite all the articles you now read, 5 percent of houses subscribe to an on-line service and 95 percent don't. So there's still a lot of opportunity for growth."

The information infrastructure is the broadest concept that builds on the evolving mix of goods and services that embody various aspects of digital convergence. It has been described as "all of the facilities and instrumentalities engaged in delivering and disseminating information throughout the nation," including facilities under public and private control for the mass media (traditionally broadcasting, cable television, and newspapers); point-to-point communications (traditionally telephone and telegraph); and associated information appliances.[5] In the present report, the term "infrastructure" is used in this general sense to include all types of information technologies, with emphasis on delivery systems (including set-top and other access-facilitating devices as well as communications facilities).

Digital convergence is important to industrial competitiveness. Computing, telecommunications, and entertainment are singular examples of U.S. strength in export as well as domestic markets—entertainment alone generates some $6 billion in export revenue, the fourth largest source of exports (behind defense, aircraft, and agriculture), with Hollywood producing 85 percent of the world's exports of theatrical and television programs (Flaherty, 1994). They also represent activities that transcend the specific industries identified by the supply of associated goods and services—the economic impacts of computing and communications show up in the performance of those who use these technologies, and much that falls under more mundane labels, such as news, can be seen as—and, increasingly, is packaged as—entertainment. Entertainment adds emphasis on creation of content to the more basic themes of productivity and other economic benefits characteristic of earlier discussions of computing and communications technologies.

To help gain perspective on the impact of digital convergence on U.S. competitiveness, the Computer Science and Telecommunications Board of the National Research Council sponsored a one-day colloquium in June 1993. The colloquium examined how digital convergence was taking shape and what economic, social, and legal issues are arising as a result of this set of changes in technology and associated industries. Participants included representatives of the computer, telecommunications, and entertainment industries; diverse government agencies; the Congress; academia; trade associations; and the media—stakeholders and independent analysts participated.[6] The steering committee sought to construct colloquium panels with a more diverse set of perspectives than those typically aired in today's press or in other venues such as industry conferences and academic conferences.

This report presents the principal insights and perspectives offered by colloquium participants. It relates colloquium discussions to events and observations that developed over the ensuing year and a half. Supplementary materials were used to augment or amplify points made by the participants and are referenced. In addition, selected colloquium participants and other experts were interviewed in mid- to late-1994 to assess whether (and if so, how) views had changed. The colloquium steering committee, through its deliberations before and after the event, completed the interpretation of key issues. Due to the limited time and space available, this report provides only an introduction to this very complex topic. However, the content is selected and organized with the intent of framing issues relevant to public policy.

The remainder of this chapter describes the state of digital convergence, including visions of the future, new private-sector alliances, and the emergence of public- and private-sector efforts to foster advances in information infrastructure. Chapter 2 outlines directions in technology and aspects of the entertainment industry. Chapter 3 addresses social issues that shape and derive from digital convergence. Chapter 4 outlines policy issues and obstacles related to promoting competitiveness and the evolution of the information infrastructure.

VISIONS AND REALITY

The early forms of interactive multimedia are only the primitive precursors of diverse technologies that even now are transforming the way many Americans live and work. Colloquium participants offered an assortment of visions and insights into how to realize the potential of such technologies.

Richard Notebaert, chairman of Ameritech Corporation, outlined a vision of broad-based benefits. Noting that 40 million personal computers were shipped in 1992, Notebaert said these "islands of intelligence" need to be interconnected so that their capabilities can be exploited fully. The availability of low-cost, high-quality digital scanners means that information from libraries, shopping malls, catalogues, and government agencies can be digitized and made available to all, he said. "What we need to do is take the technology that is available and exploit it to be part of the solution side of societal ills in this country."

Economist and author George Gilder predicted that small, portable devices with computing and communications capabilities will become indispensable. "The most common personal computer of the next decade is going to be a digital cellular phone," he said. "It's going to be as mobile as a watch, as personal as a wallet. It will recognize speech, navigate streets. It will collect your mail, open your door, and do a great variety of functions that we can't really anticipate today. And there will be a great variety of these PDAs [personal digital assistants]." Ginn, now head of a Pacific Telesis spinoff, AirTouch Communications,[7] showed a Pacific Telesis video depicting life in the year 2005, when the average citizen may have access to video telephones, PDAs, long-distance medical care and education, electronic yellow pages, and electronic libraries.

Like most colloquium participants, Ginn remarked on the difficulties and uncertainties associated with realizing the various visions of the benefits promised by digital convergence. Economist and economic historian Paul David of Stanford University observed that visions, while constructive, can blind people to near-term, practical impediments to implementing technological advances:

> Private investors and public decision makers are correct in thinking that they disregard at their peril the real hazards of a condition . . . described as technological presbyopia . . . . It's a form of far-sightedness which, in this case, makes it impossible to focus clearly on the existence of many immediate problems. It causes the sufferer to gaze too exclusively on the imagined bounties of a distant future. And to do so risks overlooking how long it will likely take to get from here to there, especially when the "there" is defined in terms of the acceptance of novel, complex consumer goods by mass markets or the pervasive adoption

of distributors' systems of production, which require significant investments in fixed capital assets by many parties.

David's caution reflects the history of technological innovation, described by Anthony Oettinger (1993) as an "anarchic, apparently tail-chasing, yet evolutionary process" that generates both ecstasies and agonies:

> The heroic and dedicated early adopters who dwell at the frontier outposts of innovation combine new tools, new information conventions, and new skills to create apparent wonders. The entrepreneurial imaginations fired up by the wonders of the early adopters promise those wonders to the prosaic, fickle old-time dwellers of the comfortable hinterlands as a wealth of new applications that never could have existed within the old confines. Hence the ecstasy. But some products and services will be ripe, others only hype. Some products and services will be ripe but unwanted. Others will be seen as too complex; still others as too simple. And the ones successful at the expense of someone else's market often enrage the losers into political action that changes the rules of the marketplace. Hence the agony.

We are in the midst of a long period of experimentation aimed largely at determining what technological possibilities are also economically viable. The experimentation evident today continues a long-term process; since the early 1980s there have been many "wired city" projects in many locations that did not work as planned yet generated significant incremental accomplishments in terms of infrastructure development and insight into demand for different kinds of entertainment (Dutton et al., 1987).

Consistent with history and despite considerable and often highly publicized market testing and formation of new ventures, the telephone, cable, and entertainment industries still concentrate their resources on traditional technologies. Their caution is due in part to uncertainty over where wealth will be generated— uncertainties that themselves reflect economic, legal, and regulatory as well as technical developments and conditions. Will there be a central component of the evolving information infrastructure, and if so, will it be a telephone, computer, cable, or wireless network, or perhaps some combination? Will information services catering to the masses ever be profitable, or will significant public investment and private contributions be needed to assure both public access and the flow of public-service information for which markets may never fully develop?

The more elusive questions pertain to what people might pay to do with emerging technologies—the word "content" becomes a kind of fetish naming this empty space without beginning to fill it. It is impossible to predict, for example, what new forms of content may emerge; new possibilities for delivering content provide greater assurance for predicting that some new forms may not be centrally generated and packaged for consumers (as is common today).

NEW PRODUCTS AND ALLIANCES:
INDUSTRIAL CONVERGENCE?

Each of the principal industries associated with digital convergence is characterized by different processes of technological and product evolution. The computing and communications industries focus on delivery and tend to be technology-driven, although recent ventures and acquisitions by Microsoft Corporation, including its acquisition of the rights to display a number of famous artistic images, illustrate the possibility for new, direct combinations of content, communications, and computing that are motivated by the computer industry (hardware and software) culture.[8] Meanwhile, the entertainment industry, with more control over content as well as a growing emphasis on delivery channels, regards both computing and communications as tools or means to an end. Whether or when an audience large enough to be economically viable will emerge to consume the new services and programs is unknown. As a Viacom executive was quoted as saying, "The technology is all there. What's missing is the consumer and exactly what the consumer wants and what they'll pay for."[9]

Although a flurry of industry announcements following the colloquium made it seem as if developments were accelerating through 1993 and early 1994,[10] subsequent events, including the failures of proposed alliances and delays in delivery of planned products, illustrated the perhaps obvious point that true, fundamental change takes time. Most startling of all was the announcement in October 1993 that Bell Atlantic Corporation, another regional Bell company, planned to buy Tele-Communications Inc. (TCI), the largest U.S. cable company, which would constitute one of the largest corporate mergers ever. The proposed merger received considerable fanfare; typical if breathless were remarks from an article in the *New York Times* (Fabrikant, 1993):

> The merger is of stunning significance because it creates a gargantuan company with both the financial wherewithal and the management skills to chase the holy grail of home information and entertainment possibilities: a vast panoply of programming and information offerings that are available at the flick of a wrist whenever a consumer wants to see them.

The two companies' plans were not consummated, leading to wholesale reassessment in the media, by investment analysts, and in the business community generally about the merits of such deals. The later demise of plans by Southwestern Bell Corporation and Cox Enterprises Inc. further underscored questions about cable-telephone company alliances (Ziegler and Robichaux, 1994).

Quoting again from Ginn's remarks at the colloquium,

> My sense is that as we begin to sort these things out, we're going to have about five years of utter confusion. You're going to see a lot of alliances. You're going to see some divorces. You're going to see the industry sort itself out among people who provide programming, who provide telecommunications, who provide cable, who provide the underlying technology to offer these services. There will be a lot of experimentation.

Steven Wildman, director of the Program in Telecommunications Science at Northwestern University, suggested in a late-1994 interview that the many approaches and separations between potential business partners reflect a pattern of movement that companies hope will leave them in the right place once that becomes apparent.

The shifting industrial landscape reflects several underlying trends. Most obviously, given their large size, telephone companies are scrambling for growth opportunities and diversification. The traditional telephone business is stagnant at perhaps a 3 percent growth rate, and these companies face possible loss of customers and/or profitability as their traditional monopolies vanish and as problems of excess capacity—constraining profitability—persist or grow. The telephone network has been relatively low cost in part because of slow depreciation, which may not be consistent with the rapid depreciation needed to deploy multiple advances in the information infrastructure, and the relatively high levels of automation and standardization of installation, maintenance, service order fulfillment, and other operations may be difficult to sustain in an environment with rapidly changing and more diverse technologies, services, and applications. Similarly, broadcasters are facing challenges from digital direct broadcast satellite and soon-to-be-digital cable and fiber television services.[11] Meanwhile, the cable industry is fragmented—some 11,000 systems owned by some 1,700 independent operators are spread across the country, lacking scale economies for effective competition against telephone companies in many instances (Samuels, 1994b). It is hard to predict the result of a situation in which, for example, both regulated and nonregulated providers of voice and video services seek to use the same technology and serve the same target markets, despite differences in approaches to standards, market share, pricing, and so on.

Despite the raising of expectations and ambitions in many quarters, the mere fact that new business activity or alliances have been launched does not mean that industries are truly converging; that would require significant shifts in industry cultures that will take a long time to achieve, as well as changes in fundamental technologies and in consumer behavior. Although much of the discussion about digital convergence seems to focus on the development of a delivery infrastructure for entertainment and other products, many challenges remain for joining the diverse cultures of computing, communications, and entertainment to make as well as deliver globally competitive products.[12] As Wildman observed when interviewed, at the very least evolution and adaption are likely within each segment in response to new tools, product concepts, and distribution possibilities.

How may dissimilar industries, which must cooperate on research and development and agree on how to implement technical solutions in standards, be joined? The computing, communications, and entertainment industries—themselves aggregates of rather different component industries—share certain characteristics, such as rapid growth in selected areas, but they are quite different in terms of structure, size, regulatory tradition, corporate culture, and the expertise they can contribute to digital convergence. For example, in terms of approach to information services, the telephone industry focuses on installing intelligence at the heart of the network. By contrast, the computer industry focuses on developing computer-based devices that can use intelligence at the periphery of networks—an orientation epitomized in the design and use of the multinational computer network known as the Internet, which is itself an application of the underlying telephone circuits in its backbone and various access networks. Nevertheless, like the computer industry, the telecommunications industry and several segments of the entertainment industry have for years depended on computer-based equipment and software for a variety of operations. This internalization of common technological elements is fundamental to manifestations of convergence in product, process, and corporate innovations.

To hedge their bets, some companies, such as AT&T, have invested in virtually every emerging information technology, although not all of the investments or plans have endured.[13] (AT&T is even getting back into the local telephone business, having purchased McCaw Cellular Communications, the largest U.S. cellular company; see *The Economist,* 1993a). However, very few companies have the resources to hedge so broadly. Others pursuing a vertical integration strategy may focus on specific segments. Sony Corporation, for example, has emphasized creating software and making machines to bring it into the home, but not the transmission of the programming (Lubove and Weinberg, 1993). By contrast, Time Warner and NewsCorp have investments in both programming and delivery systems.

Some of the joint ventures bring together all three industries—telecommunications, computers, and entertainment—for example, the formation of Prodigy Services by IBM and Sears. Another example is the diverse and international group of computing and communication companies that invested in General Magic Inc. to develop software for wireless communicators.[14]

Some alliances demonstrate how technology is lowering the boundaries between industries. US WEST Inc. put down $2.5 billion for a 25 percent share of Time Warner Entertainment (a unit of Time Warner), and NYNEX Corporation invested $1.2 billion in Viacom Inc. (*Washington Post,* 1993). Although there has been conspicuous activity among telephone companies buying into cable systems outside their service areas, interaction between telephone and cable companies underscores how what is technically possible becomes confounded by what is legally feasible and economically attractive (Kim and Wloszczyna, 1993).

The Time Warner Full Service Network experiment illustrates the complicating factor of evolving technology. The day before the colloquium, cable operator and entertainment supplier Time Warner Inc. and high-performance workstation maker Silicon Graphics Inc. announced a joint field trial to deliver video-on-demand services in Orlando, Florida—a major two-way interactive network implementation. Several months later, however, the partners announced delays attributed to technological difficulties associated with developing the necessary software and combining computing and cable technologies in an arrangement involving video servers and special set-top boxes (developed by Scientific-Atlanta Inc.; Robichaux and Clark, 1994). Actual service began in December 1994 (Shapiro, 1994).

The electronic game arena may be a bellwether for a variety of corporate and product developments. Electronic games are increasingly available over networks, but the principal market has been for access through special platforms (e.g., Nintendo and Sega systems) and on general-purpose devices, including personal computers and CD-ROM players, plus various hybrid devices, such as that offered by 3DO.[15] AT&T, Time Warner, and Matsushita Electric Industrial Company backed the company 3DO, which in early 1993 unveiled its design for an "interactive multiplayer," a CD-based machine that hooks up to a television set and combines graphics, text, and high-quality sound. The 3DO venture epitomizes the uncertainties characterizing the digital convergence marketplace. Although over 300 software developers were estimated to have begun developing programs for the 3DO platform, a new type of game system challenging others that were already established, were available at a substantially lower initial system cost, and offered yet more software was risky. In late 1994, 3DO scaled back significantly.[16]

Some observers have questioned the wisdom of huge investments in a multimedia future that has yet to prove its market value. This caution surfaced in corporate finance circles early in 1994 in the wake of the termination of the Bell Atlantic/TCI merger plans (Ziegler, 1994c). The telephone industry in particular, having built its reputation on conservative reliability, is seen by some to be abandoning its core business and character, assuming the style of Hollywood movie studios in gambling on huge payoffs in unknown territory.[17] Observed Robert Lucky of Bell Communications Research in a late-1994 interview,

> In the past 3 years the telco role has gone from doing nothing to doing everything, to something in the middle right now. . . . So far, the telcos have not been terribly successful or aggressive, I'd say, in cutting deals with the content providers, so that their role has been more that of providing a delivery vehicle. But what's changed in these last 3 years is the reality of telcos being in the video delivery business. . . . If you went back 10 years to the breakup of AT&T, nobody saw entertainment as the big plum where the big bucks were. But it's only in the last 3 to 5 years that suddenly that has become the place where the new opportunities are.

Currently, ventures appear to be small relative to the telephone companies' size, and not especially integrated into core operations or operating styles; similarly, cable company-based ventures appear to extend more traditional business patterns for the most part (Markoff, 1993).

An added complication is the difficulty in assessing what the real investment requirements may be. The discussion of the anticipated improvements in network (facilities) aspects alone, which imply huge investments in physical plant (cable and switching), marks a contrast with the investment associated with distributing information in print forms, commented John Blair of the Raytheon Corporation at the colloquium. High initial fixed costs, noted Paul David, are characteristic of the economics of network industries. On the other hand, as noted by Lucky, industry estimates for the cost of installing fiber have fallen over time—apparently due to the combined effects of competition and political jockeying.

CONCLUSION

Numerous obstacles must be surmounted in developing and assuring access to new information technologies, as well as in promoting positive consequences of their use over negative ones. Some of the problems are technical: for example, high-bandwidth, two-way communications systems are neither cheap nor widely available; there is a multiplicity of standards for representing raw information, while lack of consensus exists on standards for integrating services across different systems, a problem that threatens to grow as new interfaces proliferate. New technical bottlenecks are appearing, since video- and image-rich interactive communications require new systems, communications, and storage architectures.

On the other hand, technologists and industry analysts agree that the most critical problems are nontechnological, and also more diffuse. Digital convergence is generating a host of economic, regulatory, legal, cultural, and social issues. The atmosphere in which these issues must be resolved is chaotic and volatile; the rise of expectations for and the ultimate failure of proposed telecommunications reform legislation during the 103d Congress is but one illustration of the uncertain policy environment—itself affected by disagreements between companies, industry groups, and various other interests.

This report puts the technological and business trends associated with digital convergence into a larger framework. It seeks to advance what must be a long-term process of relating commoditization and convergence of digital electronics, communications, and entertainment products to changes in the nature of the economy and the social fabric. The intention is to provide a sense of the scope and the pace of changes transforming a set of important industries, identify some of the potential short- and long-term social and economic impacts, and frame the policy issues and dilemmas that are going to have to be resolved for all of us, whether directly or indirectly involved.

NOTES

1. According to one estimate, home shopping via television, which has $3 billion in annual sales (after some 10 years), could reach $25 billion per year by the end of the decade if the shift to sales of up-scale products succeeds. This is still only a fraction of the $245 billion in apparel and jewelry sales realized in 1993 but will likely be retail's

fastest-growing sector. Obstacles include high return rates from dissatisfied customers and the possibility that only commodity items will sell over TV, not higher-quality items (McMurray, 1994).

The medium is still dominated by down-scale products such as off-brand jewelry and clothing. A first hurdle for new networks is obtaining channel space on cable systems (Reilly, 1994).

2. A Dataquest survey found that 45 percent of 200 firms had annual revenues under $100,000; 90 percent had fewer than 50 employees (Kruger, 1994).

3. See Weber (1994). News articles differ considerably in how on-line service subscribership is reported—Prodigy Services, for example, is reported as having between 1 million and 2 million customers—but they do point consistently to negligible profits among the larger firms, including Prodigy, CompuServe, GEnie, and America Online (Lewis, 1994a,b; Ziegler, 1994b; Samuels, 1994c; *Washington Post,* 1995). On the other hand, smaller, niche-oriented on-line services, such as the Well, are reportedly profitable.

4. By the end of 1993, the installed base of CD-ROM drives in U.S. homes was 7 million and was projected to reach 16 million by the end of 1994 (Samuels, 1994a).

5. Egan and Wildman (1992) citing NTIA (1991).

6. Due to a scheduling conflict with a major industry conference, no representatives of the cable television industry were able to attend the colloquium; their perspectives on key issues were solicited in the months following the meeting.

7. The spinoff was approved by California regulators in November 1993 (Sims, 1993).

8. See Hudson (1995). See also Zachary (1994): Microsoft announced plans to buy Softimage (Montreal), a leading supplier of movie special-effects tools, for $130 million in stock. "In a recent interview, Microsoft Chairman William Gates said that the company was vigorously pursuing growth opportunities in the so-called multimedia field, where sound, images, and moving pictures are meshed together with the help of computers and software."

9. "The hard part is figuring out just which of these and a plethora of other services people want—and how to design them so they are as easy to use as television and yet bring improvements that are tangible enough so that people will pay for them" (Andrews, 1993).

10. The trade newsletter *Digital Media* identified 348 alliances in multimedia services (Laderman et al., 1993).

11. In Flaherty (1994) the senior vice president for technology at CBS described progress toward HDTV. CBS is also reported to be the first network to begin conversion to digital broadcasting. CBS plans to use Hewlett Packard video broadcast servers, including software that controls scheduling commercials and programming (McCoy, 1994).

12. Executives from at least two entertainment conglomerates (Walt Disney Co. and MCA) have expressed disdain for interactive media, and even among the players committed to some level of development there is a persistent assumption that the new technology will displace traditional forms of entertainment. Executives made the same assumption 20 years ago, when they took manufacturers of video cassette recorders to the U.S. Supreme Court with the argument that the traditional movie business would end if customers could view movies at home. That construct requires a belief that consumers are trapped in a compartmentalized universe where it is inconceivable to go to a movie theater *and* rent a video, play a video game *and* read a novel. Meanwhile, regional

rivalries have emerged among multimedia communities: Los Angeles argues pop culture is key, New York sees publishing and information as models, San Francisco is technically oriented, and Seattle follows Microsoft's lead (Shrage, 1994).

13. AT&T's Consumer Products Group dropped plans to market a modem (called "The Edge") designed to connect Sega game players' equipment via phone. Earlier, AT&T had dropped plans for 3DO-compatible gear. "AT&T executives said Consumer Products will aim its investments instead at 3 product areas: digital wireless phones, where it has been deficient against mounting competition; phones for foreign markets; and intelligent phones for the home that the company plans to begin marketing next year" (Keller, 1994).

14. Investors include Apple Computer, Motorola Inc., Sony Corp., AT&T, Matsushita Electric Industrial Co. (owner of MCA Inc. and its Universal Studios), and Philips Electronics NV. See Hill and Yamada (1993).

15. Video games are now about a $6.5 billion business. Lee Isgur, of a San Francisco investment bank: "You can talk all you want about the electronic highway and video on demand, but the only place anyone has ever sold anything interactive is in games." Over the past seven years, Nintendo and Sega have sold [over] 64 million machines in the United States. Their tack is to sell hardware cheap and license the software (classic bundling). See Tetzeli (1993).

16. The saga of 3DO is chronicled in *The Economist* (1993b) and in Turner (1993b). See also Pitta (1993), Carlton (1994d), King (1994), and Markoff (1994).

17. The enormous risk of venturing into this unknown territory, particularly in collaboration with Hollywood executives, can be illustrated by a review of foreseeable changes in the entertainment business.

Established entertainment centers (i.e., Los Angeles, New York) are no longer secure in their hegemony. In the next few decades, they will find that the dominance associated with physical concentrations of specialists, facilities, and mystique will be subject to profound change in the developing digital convergence matrix. Location-independent communities, improving microprocessor-based production tools and methods, and the rapid dissemination of many skills in expanding world markets, all undermine centrality. Just as "Detroit" is a metaphor, so it will be with "Hollywood" also.

As fresh waves of creative people struggle for access to the ballooning field, they will be far less bound to past organizational structures and practices (e.g., major studios, unions, traditional communities of the like-minded). Although this industry has a century's experience with change and readjustment, digital convergence exacerbates the process by another order of magnitude. The increasing pressure of new recruits and the human resources conflicts they engender will increase the level of disorder just enough to suggest a new chapter on chaos theory.

Meanwhile, it is clear that the corporate culture interface has been a low-priority topic in planning for digital convergence. Sooner or later, computer and telephone companies will have to confront the implications of collaborating with entertainment moguls whose market studies have all the reliability of the average shaman's chicken bone readings, in spite of the Armani suits.

2

Trends and Directions

Although it is premature to predict which technologies and applications will succeed, general directions in underlying technologies can be discerned. This chapter outlines prospects in multimedia and interactive technologies and explores applications, particularly in entertainment and education. Not intended to be comprehensive, this chapter aims to depict the fluidity of the technologies and the uncertainty of the trends they are motivating.

THE OUTLOOK FOR MULTIMEDIA
GOODS AND SERVICES

Enabling interactive multimedia to flourish are rapid advances in computer hardware, driving changes in telecommunications and other industries. Relevant hardware includes basic devices (e.g., microprocessors, memory chips and other storage devices, drives, access devices), larger computer systems that use those devices (e.g., personal computers, telecommunications switches), and other information appliances (e.g., television systems, set-top boxes).

Advances in hardware performance (and consequent reductions in the cost required to achieved any given level of performance) as measured in quantitative terms will continue to be made at very rapid rates. In the past 30 years, for example, the density of integrated circuits has improved by a factor of 10 million—seven orders of magnitude![1] Such incredible progress in such a short period of time has led to significant changes in the kinds of products that can be built from such powerful components. This rate of improvement is expected to continue at least until the turn of the century, when complex microcircuits may contain hundreds of millions of transistors, David Nagel, senior vice president and general manager of AppleSoft, said.

In a very real sense, convergence has been enabled by advances in digital hardware technology, which have in turn been driven by development of engineering processes that result in the ability to etch more and finer lines on crystals of silicon. Better lithography and more lines per millimeter enable the creation of greater and greater numbers of the active elements of digital signal processing—transistors—on any given area of silicon. One of the early pioneers of the integrated circuit, Gordon Moore (now chairman of Intel Corporation), coined a heuristic that describes the doubling in this ratio that has occurred almost like clockwork for the past 25 years, a heuristic now known as Moore's Law (Karlgaard, 1994). Having more and smaller transistors on a single chip of silicon allows those transistors to be operated at lower voltages and with lower switching currents. This in turn allows the transistors to be operated faster and at lower electrical power levels, with the net result that the microprocessors that have evolved from the earliest 10-transistor integrated circuits now have computing speeds measured in hundreds of millions of instructions per second. At these speeds, real-time multimedia computing becomes possible; advanced compression algorithms that can reduce the required bandwidth of communication systems can be implemented with circuits at price points compatible with mass markets.

Although physical laws limit how small lines can be made using the current optical lithographic technologies (a limit that would be reached shortly after the end of this century), new technologies using shorter-wavelength etching beams (e.g., x-ray, plasma) that allow significant progress below the limits imposed by visible-light lithography are now in early prototyping stages. However, new tools of all sorts are also needed to manage the incredible complexity of circuits that contain tens or hundreds of millions of switch elements. While design tools are being developed that can automate much of the design, a new problem has arisen for which no immediate solution is apparent: How does one adequately test these circuits? But while the problems of designing and testing of massively complex chips representing the very fastest hardware systems may begin to slow progress by the end of the decade, it certainly will be possible to create systems with the computing performance of today's fastest chips and all that is needed to put a complete computer on a single chip by the end of this decade. These general-purpose computing systems—complemented by more limited purpose logic for performing tasks such as high-speed compression, decompression, and even recognition of audio signals—will enable engineers to build digital systems with the overall computing power of today's supercomputers in products priced like commodity consumer electronics. In fact, the term "computing," which implies numerical computation—arithmetic—no longer adequately describes products currently being designed and sold based on high-performance digital technology.

Thus, quantitative improvements in process and component technologies have led to qualitative differences in the products built from them. One significant change has been the creation of products described as multimedia personal computers (PCs)—"multimedia" in this context emphasizing the real-time creation, processing, and presentation of sound and still and moving images or video. As discussed in Chapter 1, multimedia computing has enjoyed a rapid ascendancy in the marketplace, since images and sounds can in many situations be more efficient than text for transmitting information to humans. Today, multimedia PCs outsell by a wide and growing margin personal computers without the ability to manipulate sound and video.

For multimedia computing to be practical for products associated with mass markets, microprocessors have had to evolve to the point that they are capable of executing millions of instructions per second. Equivalent advances in memory and mass storage have also been key, because information in the form of high-resolution images may contain tens or even hundreds of megabytes of information in typical electronic publishing scenarios.

Illustrating the impact of advances in hardware is the digitization of video generation and delivery, accelerating and enhancing the coding and decoding of video signals, including associated compression of video signals (necessary for all digital delivery formats, including cable, wireless, or packaged media). Compression is important for expanding the capacity to deliver a variety of telecommunications services over a given infrastructure (e.g., a network provided by a telephone company or cable systems operator) and to increase the flexibility for a company to offer different packages of services (possibly obtained from different vendors) to different target audiences (Hodge, 1995). Costs, quality, and trade-offs between the two are changing with advances in the fundamental technology. For example, signal processing on a microprocessor chip may obviate the need for larger amounts of special-purpose hardware supporting multimedia applications; at least one such product has been announced.[2] Major computer systems and workstation manufacturers have meanwhile been developing and targeting higher-end systems as engines for video-on-demand services and associated market tests by cable and telephone companies.

Experience with CD-ROM technology, popular for storage and retrieval of multimedia products, provides some insight into the current market. CD-ROM refers to a high-capacity compact disk that can store text and video as well as sound. The number of interactive CD players in U.S. homes has been growing dramatically as a result of declining cost and proliferating software. Estimates of hardware sales and the installed base vary, but overall (homes and businesses), some 4 million CD-ROM players were sold in the United States in 1993, and the installed base in 1994 was expected to grow to 10 million to 16 million (Landis, 1993; Johnson, 1993; Flynn, 1994; Samuels, 1994a).

Despite this growth and apparent potential, consumers have voiced dissatisfaction with the problems of configuring or affording PC technology to use CD-

ROMs satisfactorily, and also with the quality of the CD-ROM software available (Carlton, 1994b). These problems, while possibly temporary and typical of relatively new technology (and expansion into a relatively unsophisticated consumer market), raise questions about consumer acceptance and about the durability of the format over time unless early problems are solved quickly and affordably. At a minimum, there is a need to improve data rates—which affect the quality of the video image that can be accessed, storage capacity, digital data reading technologies (e.g., through new laser techniques; Rosen, 1993), and response time for interactive uses (Carlton, 1994c). As Esther Dyson of EDventure Holdings Inc. observed in a late-1994 interview, enhanced speed will be an important factor in gaining broader applicability and consumer acceptance.

In the next several years, even greater performance and higher levels of circuit integation will enable the development of products that have all of the capabilities associated with multimedia personal desktop computers today but that are much different in design and function from the PCs typically found in homes, schools, and offices. Based on established trends, we can expect several lines of development.

In one, characterizable by miniaturization and mobility, we will see the functions of desktop systems available in devices the size and weight of today's electronic calculators. Products of this sort[3] will be made possible because (as noted above) as circuits of a given level of performance can be made smaller and smaller they can be made to consume less and less electrical power—and thus can be made battery powered and portable. High-performance wireless digital communication systems—packet radio, infrared, digital cellular, and so forth—have also been enabled by the general evolution in hardware technology.

In a second line of development, the object is not so much to reduce the size and increase the portability of devices as to reduce the cost. In this category will be found digital television and other products that have been described as digital information appliances. Key to the commercial success of such products is the achievement of manufacturing costs in the range of those for other kinds of appliances—roughly a factor of 10 less than the costs associated with today's personal computer products. Such improvements are achievable well before the end of the decade because it will be possible to shrink the entire circuitry associated with high-performance multimedia PCs today to a single integrated circuit. One indicator of this progress is the introduction of PC-based devices including functions historically found in radios, televisions, telephones, answering machines, and fax machines (Associated Press, 1994).

The addition of a central processing unit—a computer—could enable televisions to select a personalized viewing schedule, automatically record material, and provide memory in a hard disk, random access memory, or other solid-state device (Rosen, 1993). Development of such technologies is under way.[4] These innovations not only store programming but also meet an important emerging need, offering consumers assistance (often referred to as "navigation") in sorting through the expanding range of choices. This type of information processing/ systems integration service illustrates the contention for consumers that is emerging between televisions and more general-purpose appliances, specifically PCs. While PCs may come to play a greater role within the household, computers may proliferate within the household without looking like computers—they may be increasingly embedded into consumer electronics.[5] What may continue to differentiate appliances called computers is their general-purpose nature, including their expected use with a wide range of software, while more specialized appliances may run more specialized software.

One product that has been widely discussed is the consumer product associated with interactive television systems, a digital version of the so-called set-top box (STB). The first product that could be legitimately termed a digital STB has already appeared in the consumer market in the form of a decoder for digital satellite television broadcasts. While only weakly interactive, since digital satellite today supports high bandwidth only in the outbound direction (the current systems allow "inbound" or customer response by virtue of an analog phone connection in the back of the product), these products clearly point the way to the future.[6]

The communications companies and the entertainment industry have all become actively interested and involved in the development of both the infrastructure (see "Networks" section below) and the products necessary to enable creation of interactive television. But the key to commercial success for interactive television depends on the ability to design and manufacture inexpensive STBs (or comparable television set components). Based on historical rates of improvement, we can anticipate that the necessary technology base to support products with the performance of today's multimedia PCs and high-performance graphics workstations but with the price points of consumer electronics systems will be achievable within the next two to three years. Since interactivity will allow the creation of entertainment, communication, and other products unlike anything in the market today, these new capabilities could significantly alter the economics of all three industries: computing, communications, and entertainment.

Software

A major obstacle facing multimedia developers is the scarcity of appropriate—compatible and consumer-desirable—software. Software products are proliferating, ranging from crude translations from a traditional medium (e.g., print) to more innovative (if experimental) designs that challenge or provide a sense of control to the user (such as the computer game "Myst"; see Rothstein, 1994). Also lagging are software design and computer programming capabilities—reflecting shortcomings in design and method as well as engineering effort—with the result that new devices cannot be exploited fully. Software will be the key growth area in the years to come, according to Nagel, but it progresses on a slower time scale than does hardware. Explaining the centrality of software during a late-1994 interview, Richard Notebaert of Ameritech remarked, "The real question that we are faced with is not the technology. It's how we interact with the technology. How do we use point and click? How do we get voice-activated computers? The real question is in the world of software—the ability for humans to be able to use the software in a way that's as simple as dialing the telephone."

Nagel contended that two trends could bring about significant progress. The first trend is the development of object-oriented programming and component software. Today, software is monolithic. To make software distinctive, developers add new features to existing applications, creating "bloatware" that has marginal value, Nagel said. But eventually software may be sold in pieces, and users could assemble their own applications by selecting a framework and a set of components—including images, sounds, and text. This practice could invite a dramatic expansion of the software industry, allowing for more innovative applications, he said.

A second emerging trend is platform-independent software, such as, for example, software that can run on both PCs and Macintosh platforms. Developers currently write software to conform to applications programming interfaces, which are unique to each platform. The platform-independent principle should be incorporated into the national information infrastructure, Nagel said, because it would invite broad participation and innovation, which would hasten the evolution of the system. Software development tools for cross-platform systems are immature (Millison and LaGrow, 1993).

Generation of multimedia content implies a need for creativity as well as tools and technology. As with theatrical motion pictures and television programming, experimentation—which requires time and some freedom—should be expected. For example, the early motion pictures were essentially stage plays that were filmed, using stage makeup and stage acting techniques. As the producers became more familiar with the medium of film they developed new techniques that were specific to motion pictures. On the other hand, digitization in the music industry has until recently (Bermant, 1994) proceeded largely independently of creative authorship (except, perhaps, for sampling). Thus, while creative authorship, per se, may not drive technology change, it will respond to opportunities presesented by new technologies and, over time, may generate new requirements. In general, explained Steven Wildman in a late-1994 interview, the nature and mix of creative talents that provide comparative advantage to individuals and organizations will change.[7]

Skills—including those of graphic designers, film and video producers, scriptwriters, and teachers—will be needed in how to communicate in new media using digital tools. In a follow-up interview, Robert Stein commented on how evolving multimedia products call for new approaches to narrative and storytelling, approaches that will account for and anticipate the growing ability of the user or audience to control the pacing and sequencing of story elements. Similarly, in producing music products, "over the next couple of decades musicians will come to the fore with a broad set of skills. They won't just be able to sing and play the guitar; they'll be able to do that in both a visual sense like with music videos, and then also in an interactive sense. You're going to see musical presentations that are almost like mini-operas, where a CD isn't just for sound, it's also pictures and motion pictures, etc., and all under the control of the listener." At present, the nascent market means that job opportunities are small in number.[8] But colloquium participants emphasized the need for skills and insight, particularly the need for prospective authors who are bright, curious, and motivated.

Alexander Singer, a film director, said the requisite mechanical skills can be taught and learned; what is more important is innate desire:

> I have taught this stuff and it's learnable . . . . I taught film production techniques to a group of disadvantaged minority youth 25 years ago, and I was successful. Some were barely literate; a number had police records . . . . What I found is, they were hungry to have a voice, and the hunger was three-quarters of the game. Several of them found their way into the entertainment industry, got paying jobs, and do good work. The methods [for teaching] will be found. I think in terms of backgrounds, I would infinitely prefer somebody who was a thinking person and who had a background in the humanities, but who also had the capacity to be wide ranging, to anybody who had a specific skill, all of which I think is learnable.

Stein agreed, adding that such ideal students are difficult to find. "We're missing young people who have minds that are working, that have the ability to take complex subject matter and go out and wrestle it to the ground in a way that is satisfactory, and to bring it back to a broad audience in a way that makes any sense. "The schools are producing all kinds of kids with computer skills and graphic skills, et cetera. It's one in a million that seems to be able to understand what to do with those skills . . . . "

On a more practical note, Sherry Turkle, a professor of the sociology of science at Massachusetts Institute of Technology (MIT), said cross-sector partnerships are needed to provide training in software-writing skills. She offered as evidence MIT's $70 million ATHENA experiment with computers in education. The MIT faculty was to write the software in this project, on the theory that their innate intelligence and professional expertise would be equal to the task. However, the experiment demonstrated that writing appropriate software requires specialized cognitive skills and an artistic as well as a scientific approach; new skills or high-quality teamwork are required, Turkle has said.[9]

"I think you really do need partnerships [involving] people who are in the entertainment business, who are in the computer business, [where] the technologists are learning the anthropology, the cognitive science, the psychology, the sociology, or [they] are learning how to do studies of societal impact, of personal impact, of how people think about thinking, of how people use software, how people learn . . . ." Whereas special talent and training may be needed to generate commercial products, however, the Internet phenomenon also points to an alternative path: that of enhancing the infrastructure to the point that individual users and even commercial authors can develop content products without having to "program" as we now understand that art.

Networks

Building on but also paralleling advances in hardware is progress in networking. The full exploitation of advanced information technologies depends on networks that provide connectivity among input, display, processing, and storage systems dispersed within offices, buildings, campuses, cities, and beyond. From the user's perspective, networks can facilitate instant access to resources and integrated tools for collaboration, as well as more options for undertaking different kinds of activity from the home. George Gilder, for example, noted that more and more PCs are being connected to networks: the percentage of PCs that are interlinked grew from only 7 percent in 1989 to 60 percent in 1992. (Nagel suggested that this number will approach 100 percent by the end of the decade.) Improving upon and integrating various networks, advanced information infrastructure can provide a delivery vehicle, user interfaces, and interfaces among the components that make up interactive multimedia systems.

Nagel put current trends in computer technology into a larger historical context:

> Despite its young age, the computer has already gone through several wrenching and displacing changes. In the 1950s and 1960s, the mainframe computer was really the dominant paradigm or the dominant mode of interaction for computing and calculation. The mainframe was supplanted as the sort of center of gravity in the industry, both economically and intellectually, shifted to the minicomputer in the 1970s. In the 1980s, a third shift took place from the minicomputer to the microcomputer, again driven in large measure by process improvements and integrated circuit technology. Today, we appear to be poised for yet another major shift from microcomputing to perhaps intimate computing and also, to an era of ubiquitous networking or universal networking.

Nagel's emphasis on connectivity of computer-based devices and uses of networking contrasts with the current multimedia product emphasis on platforms that may be used apart from networks, notably CD-ROM players and game systems, although even these devices are being integrated into or substituted for by network-based applications.

Network-based applications facilitate interaction among people, whereas stand-alone applications emphasize interaction between people and computers. As Dyson observed, "interactive" can cover both concepts, but the distinction may be relevant to both the technology chosen and the impacts on the users. Thus, although questions have been raised about the prospects for CD-ROM applications to devolve to on-line information services, observers differ as to whether the market will shift largely to one format or the other or whether it will evolve in two tracks.

An assortment of transmission networks is now operating or under development in the United States. Each network has its strengths and weaknesses; to date, none constitutes a complete national information infrastructure, but collectively they are fragments of the foundation. Telephone companies, limited today by the existence of vast networks of twisted copper pair wiring in the local subscriber loops, are seeking ways of upgrading these low-bandwidth analog delivery systems to support digital transmission of information at rates required for display and transmission of high-resolution imagery and sound to—and from—digital STBs. Cable TV companies (multiple system operators) already possess a high-bandwidth distribution system (coaxial cable can support transmission of digital information in the range of hundreds of millions of bits per second). These systems, too, require significant upgrading if they are to support interactive television services since they were designed for transmission of analog television signals in one direction (outbound) only and lack both the necessary topology and switching or routing capabilities for two-way transmission of digital information. Both the plant and potential mix of services are changing to facilitate delivering the much-touted 500 video channels to the home that some system operators may offer, and digital servers and other digital facilities for delivery of movies on demand, interactive games, home shopping, and even telephone services. In particular, cable distribution is evolving to a combination of fiber and (for short residential links) coaxial cable, a hybrid approach also being adopted in many quarters of the telephone industry.[10] Indeed the cable industry is beginning to examine providing basic telephony services using some small fraction of the great bandwidth provided by their distribution systems.

The rapid advance of wireless technologies holds the promise that personal digital assistants and other forms of wireless communications eventually will be competitive with wired communications for a growing variety of applications.[11,12] Wireless technology is not new; television already is delivered by radio signals broadcast over the air, wireless cable (microwave radio frequencies used to deliver signals to rooftop antennas), and satellites; satellites have fostered the development of cable television, providing cable networks with an affordable method of linking thousands of cable systems. (Satellite broadcast services are growing rapidly in Europe, and U.S. satellite capacity continues to expand; NTIA, 1993.) The cellular telephone business, launched in 1984, has grown into a more than $10 billion per year business with well over 15 million customers, with continued growth expected. Growing competition, miniaturization of computer power, the imminent digitization of cellular phones (which will use the radio spectrum more efficiently than do their analog counterparts), and the low cost of establishing links to homes in comparison to fiber networks are among the factors behind this trend. The federal auctioning of licenses for personal communications systems networks should provide a further stimulus to wireless technology, application, and market development.

Expanding Bandwidth: Is There Enough?

A fundamental issue in digital convergence is how to assure sufficient bandwidth to transmit huge volumes of digital bits very rapidly, over a wide area. Video packaging and delivery require a substantial amount of storage and transmission bandwidth in comparison to simple numbers, text, or even still images. Video raises additional technical concerns related to multicast communication, quality of service, protocol support with the increasing deployment of asynchronous transfer mode (ATM), and so on.

Gilder was extremely optimistic about the technological prospects, claiming that the transmission speed of fiber-optic technology will multiply to the point that bandwidth will cost virtually nothing.[13] "That changes fiber from a replacement for copper to a replacement for air," Gilder said. "It makes possible a huge expanse of bandwidth. It means that all the various technologies that have been based on the assumptions of scarce bandwidth are deeply problematical in this next era. I think a major driving force of the world economy over the next 20 years is going to be the plummeting cost of bandwidth, of communications power. . . ." Although optimistic, Gilder did not address timing or what it takes to achieve a truly national capability in a timely manner—the kinds of issues being addressed in the context of telecommunication and information infrastructure policy debates.

The meaning of available bandwidth is not always clear. For example, the fact that a given network may carry aggregated traffic at 2.5 Gbps on its "backbone" links does not mean it will be able to transmit large numbers of simultaneous multimedia sessions that include video (or that any individual user will experience a 2.5-Gbps rate). Although some commercial networks already operate at 155 Mbps, a very high speed that remains difficult to exploit, even 10 Mbps or less to an individual user can support some very sophisticated interactive multimedia applications. But key technology goes beyond simple capacity to include the ability to reserve adequate bandwidth for a given period and use, the ability to use certain kinds of signaling in unswitched versus switched environments, and so on.

Interconnection and Interoperability

The number and variety of networks give rise to concerns about means of interconnection and functional exchange of information or interoperability. Eli Noam, professor of finance and economics at the Columbia Graduate School of Business, foresees a future "system of systems" managed by both traditional carriers and the systems integration industry, which would buy transmission capabilities and offer packages of services to consumers. This scenario would have the effect of "transforming the entire medium of communications into a system of systems in a software sense, superimposed on a physical structure of a network of networks," Noam said.

The complex of technologies, services, and systems integration activities anticipated by Noam is already in evidence in the Internet, where service development has been initiated by individuals and research teams but subsequently accelerated and diversified by commercial ventures (CSTB, 1994b). Indeed, the variety of services, service providers, and even customers is richer and the fit between supply and demand greater in the Internet than appears evident in the various interactive and other advanced television trials to date. One reason for that variety is the Internet's support for symmetrical (two-way) communications, with which individuals can supply as well as receive information or content generally and services. Whether the Internet leads or becomes subsumed in the development of a yet larger and more complex information infrastructure, the commercialization of the Internet provides a laboratory for observing the interplay of technology, business development, and ancillary policy considerations.[14]

Michael Borrus, co-director of the Berkeley Roundtable on the International Economy, offered a somewhat different prospect. He perceives a "portfolio" of networks emerging at different rates, managed separately and for different purposes. He contends that there is no ideal configuration and that flexible design permits specialized networks to meet the needs of particular user groups. All networks are evolving toward expanded bandwidth and increased intelligence, Borrus said, but each is driven by different market and policy dynamics and is evolving different applications. "Each of these . . . networks, in very different ways, requires very different degrees of privacy, of liability and the like," Borrus observed. "It isn't at all clear to me that one all-singing, all-dancing infrastructure can provide that diversity at the moment, or whether it should provide that diversity."

Borrus' reservations foreshadowed the debates that have emerged subsequently over the federal initiative to advance the nation's information infrastructure. Those debates revolve around the issue of what it means to have "a" national information infrastructure, especially if such an entity is not monolithic or homogeneous and is not financed or controlled by a single entity. Borrus' argument suggests a greater polarity of alternatives than may be feasible, especially from the perspective that the information infrastructure will grow from existing roots. CSTB has explored these issues in its 1994 report *Realizing the Information Future*, which argued the need for an overarching framework or architecture that could tolerate and accommodate multiple and competing technologies, facilities, services, and businesses as well as evolution in these elements. Multiple networks are likely to persist, given the heterogeneity of consumers and differentiation of offerings from different network providers. This multiplicity will give rise to both translation approaches (e.g., via STBs) and more direct integration of services.[15] Given the reality of diversity, a key issue for both information infrastructure and the broader phenomenon of digital convergence will be standards.

Standards

A standard is a set of technical specifications followed by manufacturers or service providers, either tacitly or as a result of a formal agreement. Standards have emerged as a theme in CSTB's series of competitiveness colloquia, but digital convergence magnifies the challenge as well as the opportunity associated with standards setting in individual technology areas or industries. A standard for a mass media product can enhance both consumer and producer welfare. The success of the Internet, for example, is attributed in part to the standards that permit the various member networks to link together. Indeed, the Internet is effectively defined by a set of standards that outline the minimum requirements for connectivity and access to associated services, the essence of interoperability.

Economic historian Paul David of Stanford University eloquently framed the importance of standards, an otherwise prosaic topic that lies at the heart of achieving convergence across both technologies and industries:

> A fully articulated vision of the future and the future shape of any complex technological system serves a crucial role in coordinating and stimulating the diverse, decentralized undertakings on the part of many actors that the successful, practical development of such systems typically requires in the context of every capitalist market economy. Standards . . . are part of the set of coordination devices which are needed to engage the activities of the suppliers of many components in developing the kinds of systems that are being discussed. But, there is also the conceptual standard, the vision, a coordinating vision which plays an important role. In the context of the evolution of network technology, it's been especially true that technological visionaries have been potent as agents of industrial progress.

As suggested earlier, consensus-based technical standards are needed in multimedia. Decisions need to be made, for example, with respect to standards for compression, which will affect how much full-motion video can be stored on a CD-ROM and how cheap or expensive it is to communicate full-motion video over different kinds of networks.[16] Other areas where approaches differ and standards may be valuable are in digital sound processing,[17] STBs, and other elements of interactive video systems (Ziegler, 1994a; Corcoran, 1994; Hodge, 1995).

When and how to establish technical standards are contentious issues.[18] Timing is critical, David observed, because setting standards too early can foreclose opportunities,[19] but waiting too long can hinder technology development.

As David noted:

A standard . . . has the properties of public knowledge. . . . It's a public good. You can't have a standard just by yourself. Other people have to be able to coordinate with it, if what you're producing is a system which has many participants forming a distributed system, and you want to have a continual process of incremental improvement and elaboration. . . . The issue of standards is not whether to have them, but timing. How soon and how long do you hang up the development in the field by not having standards, or how soon do you foreclose possible opportunities by setting standards too early? I think these are the timing questions that we should be thinking about.

Although standards may have the qualities of public goods, they may contain proprietary elements; "open," "public," and "proprietary" are not necessarily exclusive. This issue arises in a wide variety of standards relevant to digital convergence. For example, Cable Television Laboratories Inc. has proposed establishing a clearinghouse for intellectual property rights for components of the Motion Picture Experts Group (MPEG)-2 standard for digital video transmission. MPEG-2 core technology includes many different patents from companies and individuals worldwide; a reasonable, fair, and nondiscriminatory way to access such patent rights will speed adoption of an international standard. As Borrus noted, the fastest-growing products in today's electronics systems markets— whether computers, telecommunications equipment, or consumer electronics— are developed around proprietary standards that evolve rapidly in the marketplace through competition. Game companies are competing to invent the next unique platform, which, if it becomes the dominant standard, would bring its creator substantial rewards, Nagel said.[20] The reconciliation of "open" standards with proprietary technology is debated among executives and scholars.[21]

Different players in the digital convergence arena have different experiences and traditions when it comes to standard setting. Older technologies, such as televisions, fax machines, and telecommunications equipment, evolved around publicly developed standards. Standard setting here has been relatively formal and slow. In the communications arena, the Internet Engineering Task Force and the ATM Forum illustrate two venues in which standard setting has proceeded relatively quickly, belying the notion that standard setting is always very slow.

The market-contention approach to standards setting, which originated in the computer industry, is the strategy Nagel favors for advancing the national information infrastructure. "Basically," Nagel said, "the idea is that, rather than getting in a committee room and arguing about the nature of standards and the ideal standards for any given application, the practice in the personal computer industry has been for groups of engineers to get together to build systems that demonstrably work. The best of these systems eventually comprise a de facto standard." An approach based on working implementations is epitomized by Internet standard setting, which involves ratification of demonstrated technologies. When it comes to de facto standards, however, it is not always clear that the best technology wins, a point made by observers of videocassette (VHS vs. Beta) and other arenas; strategy, marketing, and other factors relating to market presence can be at least as important as "technology," per se.

This process stimulates innovation and elevates the standard, with the inventor owning and profiting from the intellectual property that defines its value, Nagel said. "I think the whole standard-setting process is becoming a lot more sophisticated . . . the telecommunications industries and the computer guys are beginning to get together [to develop standards], and it almost binds them." The process remains imperfect and contentious, however, with cultural differences as well as different technical preferences constituting impediments to more rapid resolution. Another factor is market power: in the software arena, Microsoft has sufficient market presence that its products often serve as de facto standards, a phenomenon that has motivated rival standards-oriented consortia.

One effort to keep the software and other digital convergence arenas as fluid as possible is the "open reference" platform, which has "maximized the impact of individual innovation, particularly in the software world," Nagel said. This term refers to abstract or generic software and hardware combinations, which are open in the sense that anyone can exploit them. An example is the IBM Corporation's PC, which spawned a series of "clones"; software designed for the IBM version will run on all clones. More than 600 companies now build specific products based on that concept, Nagel said.

In the entertainment industry, standards traditionally have been set either by dominant companies or through cooperative efforts;[22] the latter approach is being pursued with multimedia and other digital technologies. For example, the MPEG has developed criteria for the compression of moving audio and video (Yadon, 1993), and the cable industry makes use of MPEG-2 chip sets, anticipating economies of scale and interoperation with other digital coding applications, as in consumer electronics devices (NCTA, 1993c).[23]

Some standards for digital convergence are being developed through forums involving all three industries—computer, telecommunications, and entertainment. One avenue is the Interactive Multimedia Association, which sponsors an open forum (the Compatibility Project) to develop recommendations on cross-platform compatibility of multimedia data and applications. An issue for progress in digital convergence is the proliferation of standard-setting groups, some formed explicitly to compete with others. Even where there may be overlapping corporate membership it is not clear that people in industry *A* are fully involved in standard setting dominated by industry *B*, and so on. Further, with so many standard-setting activities, the ability of a given company, even a leader in its field, to participate adequately will be inherently limited given the need to devote time, talent, and other resources. The problem is magnified by the increasingly international nature of relevant standard setting; U.S. efforts must reflect and anticipate global deployment and competition. The nature of the standards-setting process varies somewhat across countries, and delays are compounded by the need for cross-national consensus in international standard setting. The Information Infrastructure Standards Panel launched by the American National Standards Institute in 1994, with the involvement of multiple trade, standards-developing governmental, and other organizations, represents an effort to forge a broader consensus, although the broader the group the more difficult the process of reaching consensus.

Symptomatic of the problem is the tendency of some to look to industry consolidation as a way around the standards-development problems. For example, the collapse of the proposed Bell Atlantic/Tele-Communications Inc. merger led some observers to wonder about the consequences of not having a "unified force that might have set nationwide technical and operating standards for networks delivering video-on-demand, home-shopping and high-speed data services" (Andrews, 1994b). The need for and alternatives to recognizable market leadership remain subjects for debate and analysis, although the demise of the Bell Atlantic-TCI deal is generally accepted as a sign of the slowing of the pace of both industry consolidation and technology deployment.[24] The challenge of developing standards is recognized as a pacing factor for the enhancement of the information infrastructure.

ENTERTAINMENT AND THE ENTERTAINMENT INDUSTRY

If entertainment and creative content are what differentiate digital convergence from the narrower merging of computing and communications, the entertainment industry becomes a central player. The approximately $6 billion U.S. market for home-based video games is hard evidence of the business potential from creating programming for interactive technologies. Yet such first-order product revenue estimates do not capture the larger, second-order revenues associated with service, manufacturing, and other activities. And the game market illustrates the fact that it may be hard to ascribe revenues to any one industry, since electronic/video games are offered as computer software, on-line services, and programs for special-purpose game systems, and they may draw on components derived from other products (e.g., motion pictures or television shows), giving them the character of an aftermarket product. Similar questions arise for home shopping, which—as a television offering—can be considered entertainment by some and retail distribution by others. In this instance, the differentiation of revenue passed through to product vendors from revenue associated with the delivery medium (e.g., a cable television shopping show) is important, along with determination of the extent to which new shopping activity is stimulated as opposed to diversion of shopping to the new media from more conventional ones (e.g., on-site store shopping, mail-order, or conventional catalogue and phone shopping). If, as suggested by Nagel, the way to maximize returns is to dominate a particular layer or link in the multimedia production and distribution chain, the difficult task of understanding the structure of the industry complex and how it is evolving becomes essential.

The entertainment industry is far from monolithic; it is really a set of different industries that produce such products as feature films, television programs, recorded music (records/CDs and tapes), and games. Each of these areas faces different production problems and different distribution and marketing problems. Further, individual entertainment industries have different cultures and concerns, resulting in a situation where those who work in one of these industries do not usually have much to do with the others unless there is some overlap of interests (as when the makers of theatrical motion pictures see that one can design and market games based on hit movies).

In evaluating how the new digital technologies and media interact with the entertainment industries, it is important not to generalize too much. For example, many of the technologies most heavily discussed in the context of digital convergence have to do with new methods (e.g., optical fiber cable to the home) of distributing existing products but will not make major changes in the type of product that is distributed. Thus, for example, the recorded music industry embraced digital technology some time ago but has begun to go interactive only recently.[25] Other technologies (e.g., CD-ROMs) allow for new types of products that have not previously existed—although they may be used initially to repackage traditional products (e.g., as a substitute for vinyl records) or to complement them (e.g., on-line discussion groups organized by fans of television shows; Barron, 1994).

The entertainment industry will use digital technology in the following ways: (1) as a new delivery system for existing products (e.g., video on demand), providing essentially a new aftermarket for existing products;[26] (2) in electronic games (and other ways of using digitized material, thereby increasing the variety of delivered products;[27] (3) for direct-response sales ("home shopping"); (4) for new entertainment products that are in the process of being invented (e.g., Robert Winter's musical "books" demonstrated at the colloquium); (5) for potentially new distribution systems that would allow distribution of products to audiences that are not reached today; (6) for location-based entertainment, such as "high-tech" theme parks based on visual simulation and other offshoots of both the aerospace and electronics industries; and (7) for new production methods to enhance and/or lower the costs of existing products (e.g., computer animation or using virtual reality to design set lighting, or use of nuances of sound as dramatic elements). Digitization allows for new types of special effects and production technologies, often building on technologies and applications developed for scientific research contexts (e.g., visualization), that can be incorporated into existing types of media.

Given these opportunities and possibilities, it is important to consider the differentiation between those parts of the entertainment industry complex that produce the programming (software) and those that distribute the programming that is produced. For example, in theatrical motion pictures, box office receipts compose only a part of the market, and producers look to the aftermarkets (foreign, videocassette, sale to television (pay, network, and syndication)) to show a profit. The production of television programming is a deficit business: to cover its production costs, a TV program needs to be sufficiently successful to stay on the air for some 65 episodes, a threshold for sale to syndicated television. The issues facing these two areas of production are different from those facing the cable television owner or the over-the-air broadcaster that distributes the programming already produced.

Another distinction pertains to those who wish to distribute existing types of programming in a digitized format and those who wish to create new types of programming using digital methods. The former category allows for a broader concept of the entertainment industry, one that would embrace cable television operators and computer network operators and possibly telephone companies, for example, as well as possible changes in the role of movie theater operators. Consider, for example, group interactive electronic games, which provide a new form of distribution. They may employ large-screen, sophisticated computer-graphic imaging, and programming at a level of narrative complexity and character depth well beyond that available in current video and arcade games. Developments in interactive storytelling concepts alongside advances in computer software and hardware are evolutionary corollaries of present systems.[28]

Although the actual "workers" in interactive media may be at secondary levels of the industry, it is clear that all major entertainment companies at their top levels have made a commitment to exploring ways that the digital convergence can interface with their products. Virtually every major Hollywood studio has established a subsidiary to create interactive products, typically computer adventures games based on movies. So far, most are repackagings of existing products, but that could change with the recent focusing of industry attention on games and the recognition that game revenues (over $6 billion per year) now exceed box office receipts (over $5 billion per year) (Siegel, 1994; Rothstein, 1994). Similarly, record components, seeing music production innovations being led by specialized multimedia (software) companies, are adding interactive media functions to their staffs (Bermant, 1994).[29,30] The new Academy of Interactive Arts and Sciences has been established to confer awards in the field, the Houston International Film Festival has established new prizes for interactive multimedia products, and the American Film Institute's (Apple- supported) computer-based graphics, editing, and multimedia classes are overflowing (Siegel, 1994; Turner, 1993a). The process of exploration is highly fluid and uses a wide range of information and technological dissemination, networking, alliances, seminars, schooling, capital investments, and research and development.

In terms of generating and delivering creative products generally, the United States has dominated the global mass entertainment market since the turn of the last century. "There is an accusation from almost every civilized country on Earth that America is a cultural imperialist," Singer observed. "If you talk to a Japanese anthropologist about how many pieces of Japanese electronics there are in America, he'll tell you, 'Yes, but you've captured our children. They walk around in Batman masks all over Tokyo, and UCLA T-shirts. . . .'" Similarly, Nagel has observed that daily activities in Bali have been undertaken to the accompaniment of broadcast U.S. rap music.[31]

Singer attributed this dominance to the many generations and networks of creative talent that have resided in Southern California over the years. Hollywood always has catered to a mass audience, he said, beginning with the nickelodeon, which for a nickel would entertain viewers with a womanly form, a couple kissing, the barrel of a gun, or horses or trains moving. Significantly, Japan adapted the nickelodeon for the intellectual aristocracy, Singer said.

Hollywood's inventive tradition can be traced to the unique nature of American culture, according to Singer. The nation's relative youth "gives us permission to play," and, as immigrants, Americans have an innate sense of adventure and dreams of possibilities. Moreover, Californians traditionally have been explorers; the early leaders of the entertainment industry, such as Louis B. Mayer, were itinerant salesman, Singer noted. The early influx of immigrants from other states, as well as foreigners escaping turmoil overseas, brought new ideas and excitement to Hollywood, a phenomenon that continues. Los Angeles today is characterized by "an anxious and driven spirit of reinvention," he said. See Box 2.1.

Market forces also play a role in the global dominance of the U.S. entertainment industry. Wildman said the industry is more commercial than its foreign counterparts and, furthermore, it commands not only a huge domestic market but also the worldwide market for English-language products.[32] About half of major U.S. producers' earnings from movies and television come from foreign markets,[33] and so entertainment is a major positive contributor to the U.S. balance of trade,[34] Wildman said. The large audience for U.S. video products—for which the costs of distribution are small compared to the initial cost of producing the creative product—has enabled producers to command huge production budgets, allowing them to invest heavily in entertainment value and audience appeal,[35] and thereby propelling the export advantage, he said. U.S. film producers spend some four to ten times the budgets of European counterparts, resulting in pioneering special effects (embodying digital convergence) and higher production values generally.

The introduction of new technologies is transforming the structure of the entertainment marketplace. As more outlets or channels are added, the return to each individual producer shrinks, Wildman explained. For example, the rise of cable television was paralleled by a decline in the three major broadcast networks' share of the prime-time audience (U.S. DOC, 1993). Smaller shares mean lower advertising revenues and smaller production budgets for prime-time programs, Wildman said, as evidenced by the proliferation of low-budget "reality" shows (although the impact of changes in share depends on the type of audience affected, which itself affects advertising revenues). On the other hand, the emer-

---

Box 2.1 A Message from Hollywood

Serious-minded executives may doubt they have anything to learn from Hollywood. To be sure, film director Alexander Singer acknowledged, Hollywood is a peculiar place, a land of fantasies and dreams. "There are people who wear suits and sit in an office when in fact 'visions of sugar plums dance in their heads,'" he said. "They are filled with the fantasy of boundless possibility. The brass ring of a $500 million-grossing film is so intoxicating that it leaves ordinary and sensible people dizzy with desire."

Movie makers are gamblers, taking wild chances on expensive bombs such as *Ishtar* and unexpected blockbusters such as *Home Alone.* "They do not know what it is that works," Singer said. "They cannot know. They never know." Yet, ironically, they are highly paid to know. This environment of high risk, high stakes, and relentless pressure to appear in control makes the entertainment business profoundly insecure and unstable, Singer said. Moreover, the odds against success are astronomical. For example, about 30,000 screenplays are registered every year by the Writer's Guild of America; only a few hundred are purchased, and a fraction of those are actually made into movies, he said. All of this fosters a creative atmosphere, but one with "a sickly quality . . . a sense of addiction."

This creativity is struggling to find the application to multimedia. Hollywood executives are notoriously fearful of venturing beyond the familiar; Singer found senior entertainment executives to be "conservative" and "anxious" when confronted with virtual reality technology entertainment concepts during the early 1990s. Such reactions cast doubt on the prospect of the entertainment industry serving as a model for systematic innovation.

Yet in one way the industry does serve as a prototype for survival in the information age, according to Singer, who believes Hollywood is a kind of precursor for certain forms of work forces and lifestyles of the future. A large part of this culture is one of impermanent but highly skilled production group teams. These temporary task forces, brought together for a single movie or televisions series, work intensely with a high degree of skill, quickly building personal relationships and teamwork comparable to that of a string quartet or a baseball team, Singer said. At the completion of the assignment the team dissolves and the individuals search for new employment. They are motivated as much by professional pride as by monetary gain.

These workers must be highly independent: they need to inform themselves about industry activity, network to find jobs, and upgrade their skills regularly. They also must raise families and stay sane and healthy while living this moment-to-moment lifestyle. (Time lost for illness is among the lowest in any industry.) It is a model that could serve as a useful variant for the business community, Singer said, as job impermanence comes to characterize much of American life.

---

gence of new media creates new "windows" in the distribution chain—new aftermarkets. The overall effect is to increase the aggregate audience for a given production, Wildman said.

Another transforming factor may relate to financing. For example, film industry financing changed with the introduction of sound in motion pictures.

Previously, most film production had been financed by entrepreneurial individuals working in the industry or their associates. Sound imposed serious new technical demands on filmmaking that required expensive equipment and talent, prompting Hollywood to turn to New York capital markets, which had underwritten earlier stages of the industry. This experience provided the rudiments of the current film industry's financing structure, with profound consequences for the character (both technically and in terms of content) of a major part of the entertainment industry. Thus, beyond its effect on what it is like to see a movie, sound changed the movie industry into something new, and that new thing produced different products than the old thing.[36] By analogy, the long-term effects of new digital convergence technologies may be more profound with respect to altering the traditional definition of the industry than on the industry as currently defined. Overall, a major part of that transformation may be from a goods-producing to a service-producing orientation.

Wildman also observed that as channels and programming proliferate, much of the "value added" starts to reside in the technology that allows us to sort, sample, and select what we want to use. As noted above, competing industries are offering different methods and approaches for those processes of finding entertainment content to consume.

Only technologies that provide meaningful benefits to the creative community will take hold in the entertainment industry complex. The integration of new technologies will be driven by (1) enhancing the creative tools used by the entertainment industry to create its art form; (2) demonstrating cost economies and operational efficiencies; and (3) enabling new forms of entertainment and/or innovative ways to simulate reality. For example, with its 360-degree stereoscopic computer-graphic universe, individual spatial volition, and simultaneous interacting multiple players, fully evolved virtual reality currently is the most potent and problematic technology of the whole interactive spectrum. This medium gains particular relevance in the way it reflects aspects of the "virtual communities" emerging from the computer networks (Rheingold, 1993).

Thus, while the popular and business press tout prospective impacts from greater bandwidth in communications capacity, applications of virtual reality from CD-ROMs and other new devices, and other digital convergence components and products, it remains premature to determine what difference individual developments may make. The bandwidth breakthroughs of today are impressive, but in context they may prove no more earth-shattering than earlier transformational jumps in communications capacity such as multiplexing of telephone trunk circuits or transformations in entertainment such as the addition of sound and color to film. The changes brought about by today's instances of digital convergence may be changes in degree or in kind; some may be changes in degree that are so significant as to be changes in kind. Ginn contended that ability to satisfy audiences is more important to success than is the kind of business: "If your view is that markets will segment, and I think they will over time, then those companies that have the understanding of markets and how to satisfy customer needs, irrespective of where they are in this value chain, will be able to be very profitable. This includes cable companies and telecommunication companies and others in the distribution end."

Reinforcing Ginn's view that it is insight as much as origin that matters was the apparent confusion at the January 1994 Information Superhighway Summit, a government-industry gathering that addressed, in a group more heavily dominated by entertainment industry executives, some of the issues raised at the CSTB colloquium. As reported in the *Los Angeles Times* (Lippman and Harmon, 1994):

> Not atypically for Hollywood, the most compelling reason many gave for attending the conference was that everyone else was. For the last year, representatives of the communications and media industries have demonstrated an almost compulsive need to trade information highway metaphors at symposiums and conferences with titles such as "Digital World," "Multimedia Expo" and "Digital Hollywood." Although everyone agreed that the highway is coming—and soon—there was little consensus about how it will evolve, how much it will cost or how quickly people will be able to access it through their computers, telephones or television sets . . . . Yet members of the Hollywood crowd seemed unsure of their place in the sparring between phone, cable and computer executives over how digital age entertainment and information will be delivered. "I feel like an English major in an organic chemistry course," said Disney's [Michael] Eisner.

Notwithstanding the many ways that digital convergence can affect and be affected by the entertainment industry, there is likely to be a broader interaction with entertainment, per se. Entertainment is an essential part of human activity as well as an industrial classification signifier.[37] The latter does not encompass the former in any meaningful way. Conventional measures of activity regarding the entertainment industry reflect no more accurately on the human activity of entertainment than measures of fertilizer production reflect accurately on the state of world nutrition, obesity in the United States, or changing fashions in cuisine. Failure to see the breadth and depth of entertainment as a central element in human activity, extending into many other realms of "production," probably accounts for the consistent misprediction of growth in markets for such products as consumer electronics and such services as long-distance telephone. These markets, at least from an economic perspective, have appeared to be almost completely "supply-driven"—the economist's euphemism for the fact that no one predicted the growth that actually occurred when the market took off. Yet they clearly have tapped deeply into some fundamental demand structure. Wildly optimistic and misplaced expectations for the picture-phone and interactive television illustrate the same confusion about the real nature of entertainment. The simple fact is, we don't understand the issue of entertainment very well.

In looking for and predicting the impact of digital convergence, it may be useful to consider the potential of existing information goods and services as entertainment: newspapers are information services catering to the masses, and commercial television almost defines that concept. Commercial television news is clearly a kind of information service, reporting facts, but it is also largely an entertainment product. A significant fraction of network television news budgets come from the networks' entertainment budgets, and the proliferation of "newsy" shows with celebrity anchors shows just how profitable such "infotainment" can be. Some would even argue, a la H.L. Mencken, that government itself is a source of entertainment (certainly supported by the success of the cable television network, C-SPAN), raising questions about some fraction of political expenses (polling, campaign consultants, and other election costs) relating to entertainment. As discussed in Chapter 3, related arguments might be made—and are made, seriously—in the context of education. The question is not what will happen with the new technologies and entertainment, but rather, what will these technologies add to the technology/entertainment mix already well in place?

NOTES

1. In 1962, an integrated circuit (IC) contained 10 transistors; today, one IC contains millions of transistors.

2. "Intel Corp. and Spectron Microsystems, Inc. [plan] software that will support native signal processing on a Pentium chip, allowing multimedia software to run on the processor instead of requiring dedicated hardware . . . . The Pentium processor, though not fast enough to handle Joint Photographic Experts Group- and Motion Pictures Expert Group-type compression, will be able to compress and manipulate audio signals. This means that recorded speech can be slowed down or sped up . . . . The initial release will support audio only; video and communication will be supported later" (Mohan, 1994). A variety of specialized hardware components is used to support a variety of functions, from sound to graphics to communications, increasingly displacing specialized boxes and subsystems. Much innovation is taking place in more miniature and more integral communications componentry, for example, providing phone, fax, and voice mail capabilities within personal computers. See Corcoran (1993).

3. New terms—"personal digital assistants," "personal communicators," and the like—have already been coined to describe these products.

4. For instance, AT&T and a small company specializing in digital signal compression are developing an electronic "black box" for television set tops, to provide for reception and decoding of movies and other video services using telephone lines (Klein and Aston, 1993). Hewlett Packard and TV Answer collaborated to build a set-top box that provides interactive services; the system uses a portion of the radio spectrum to uplink and download signals from a satellite (Millison and LaGrow, 1993).

5. The overlap between computers and conventional consumer electronics was noted in connection with the newcomer role of Microsoft and Intel at the 1994 Las Vegas Consumer Electronics Show. "Their inclusion illustrates just how blurred the line has become between computers and consumer elecronics. While sales of more traditional consumer equipment languish, computer concerns hope to spur purchases of multimedia

personal computers, hand-held 'digital assistants' and sophisticated computer games" (Carlton, 1994a).

6. See Hodge (1995) for a discussion of technical and design issues for STBs that could support interactive television. Hodge asserts that an STB consistent with open architecture is "a remote control unit for the video server, to which it connects through an ATM network. This is the distinction between this unit and pre-ITV [interactive television]. It provides bilateral, full duplex communications to the video server" (p. 154).

7. Wildman commented on how the introduction of sound in film ended careers of actors with poor voices and enabled careers of actors whose voices carried well.

8. "[W]hile virtually every major publishing house and Hollywood studio has announced plans to develop sophisticated, high-quality multimedia software, and though cable, telephone and computer companies are forming alliances to test interactive TV systems, many of these ventures are in their infancy and won't translate into large numbers of jobs for years" (Kruger, 1994).

9. Sherry Turkle, personal communication, November 11, 1993.

10. With research under way in numerous technical areas aimed at leveraging its network architecture, the cable industry is billing its infrastructure as "the missing link to myriad multimedia applications," including personal communications services (Dukes, n.d.).

11. Information can be carried on electromagnetic impulses or waves in various frequencies, the sum of which is known as the spectrum. The full electromagnetic spectrum ranges from radio waves (relatively long wavelengths) to x-rays and cosmic rays (at short wavelengths). Transmission through the air is concentrated in a narrow portion of the radio spectrum; radio frequencies that are very low cannot carry enough information for video, while radio signals at high frequencies cannot penetrate objects. Competition is growing for the prime bands of radio frequencies (Chiddix, 1991).

12. A comprehensive analysis of wireless technology may be found in *The Economist* (1993a).

13. This argument hinges on the development of amplifiers that can increase the speed of fiber-optic transmission. Today, fiber-optic technology is constrained by an electronic bottleneck: every 22 miles, the signal must be converted to electronics and then regenerated, Gilder noted. This means that, despite its wide bandwidth, fiber optics is limited in speed to 2.5 gigahertz (2.5 billion cycles per second). But the true capacity of fiber optics is 25,000 gigahertz—1,000 times all the frequencies used in the air today. "It could accommodate all phone calls in America on the peak moment of Mother's Day," Gilder said.

14. Experimentation with real-time audio and video conferencing over the Internet has begun using the so-called Mbone multicast backbone (Eriksson, 1994).

15. This phenomenon is discussed in Katz and Shapiro (1994).

16. The Motion Picture Experts Group (Radcliffe, 1993) and a variety of corporate alliances and consortia (Markoff, 1995a) have pursued standards for video compression and video storage.

17. Sound systems for films with digital sound are expensive and variable. Digital Theater System places the soundtrack on a disk separate from the film and synchronizes the two. Sony Dynamic Digital puts the soundtrack on the outer edge of the film, while Dolby uses the space between sprocket holes (Fantel, 1994).

18.   An overview of the standards-setting process for information networking is provided in CSTB (1992), p. 56.

19.   For example, the standard for audio CDs is lower than current recording capabilities. The "Red Book" standard calls for music to be stored in a 16-bit format, meaning the sound is sampled at 16 places along the sound wave 44,100 times per second; by contrast, studios now can record digitally using a 20-bit system, sampling 16 times more information and creating richer sound (Herschman, 1993).

20.   See Pereira (1994) and Carlton and King (1994).

21.   The intersection of standards setting and intellectual property rights management has been tracked in the annual Telecommunications Policy Research Conference series and in a 1994 workshop on standards setting for information infrastructure sponsored by the National Institute of Standards and Technology.

22.   For instance, the de facto standard for studio film productions—35-millimeter film at 24 frames per second—has survived for more than 60 years; the "Red Book" standard for CDs was set by Philips NV and Sony Corp. (NTIA, 1993).

23.   In addition, the Multimedia and Hypermedia Experts Group is developing coding for multimedia to manage throughput on distribution networks (Dukes, n.d.).

24.   According to Farhi and Sugawara (1994), "None of the experts is suggesting that the information superhighway won't get built, just that early predictions of its quick completion were grossly overstated."

25.   A number of major artists are pursuing interactive ventures, and consumers can buy products that allow them to create music out of preconstructed parts, or experience combinations of music, art, and games (David, 1993; Goldberg, 1993; Bermant, 1994).

26.   Where material can be confined to digital formats, economies can be reaped, for example through the electronic cinema concept, reducing the need to undergo the expense of conversion of motion pictures to film (especially likely where material is produced expressly for electronic distribution rather than traditional theatres).

27.   Walt Disney Co. licensed Microsoft and Sony Imagesoft to develop multimedia titles featuring Disney characters. "Industry analysts say collaborations of this kind will proliferate as entertainment companies like movie studios seek new media to exploit for licensing revenue and as software publishers seek characters of proven appeal for interactive games and stories" (Fisher, 1994).

28.   A rare insider's perspective on the difference between storytelling structure and video games may be found in Parkes (1994).

29.   See Landis (1993), Lohr (1994), and Schwarz (1993). Multimedia projects under development by major studios include interactive cartoons; explanatory versions of old movies showing, for example, how certain dance sequences were created; a virtual biopark, which will enable children to experience an animal's lifestyle; interactive television shows, including games, dramas, and mysteries; and interactive amusement park rides.

30.   A notable late entrant was the Walt Disney Co., which initially stayed out of the multimedia technology business and instead licensed its standard programming for multimedia use. Chairman Michael D. Eisner said of interactive media, "I don't like it so we won't invest in it" (The Superhighway Summit, Academy of Television Arts and Sciences, Los Angeles, January 11, 1994). Eisner also has expressed concern that more channels will mean more mediocrity: "A real nightmare is finding out that the superhighway has turned into a detour . . ." (Laderman et al., 1993). In late-1994, however, Disney

announced plans for greater activity revolving around interactive software products (Turner, 1994b).

31.   David Nagel, personal communication, October 1994.

32.   The United States is "by far the world's most important supplier of films for international trade," Wildman has written, citing UNESCO statistics (Wildman and Siwek, 1988). These authors suggest there is a strong, positive relationship between the purchasing power of native speakers in any language—the English-speaking population happens to be wealthy and populous—and the importance of trade in films and television programs in that language.

33.   This figure comes from Wildman's analysis of a period of 30 years ending in 1988 (Wildman and Siwek, 1988).

34.   The U.S. film industry had a positive trade balance of approximately $1 billion in 1985, even though foreign earnings are reduced significantly by a number of trade barriers, as well as by piracy (Wildman and Siwek, 1988).

35.   The value of film and television products to consumers is "determined almost entirely by such public-good elements as the appeal of the story portrayed, the quality of the writing and acting, the perspective of the director, and the competence of camera crews and other technical personnel" (Wildman and Siwek, 1988). A public good is nonexclusive; that is, its value is not diminished by its use.

36.   Of course, new, foreign sources of investment may also provoke major changes in segments of the entertainment industry, but that issue was beyond the scope of this project.

37.   See Huizinga (1950) for a discussion of the role of play in society.

3

Societal Implications

Digital convergence is expected to transform every field and every aspect of U.S. society, from business and education to health care and libraries, from the structure of the nation's economy and laws to the psychology of the individual. Samuel Ginn observed: "At a minimum, [digital convergence] is going to impact how we work and play, and that is to say that it's going to affect our standard of living. Indeed, it will influence our competitiveness as a nation. It's going to influence how we relate to one another, how we educate ourselves, how we administer health care, how privacy is protected. Even the whole concept of national sovereignty is going to have to be dealt with."

Advanced communications services, fostered by digital convergence, are seen by many as key contributors to social and economic prosperity (Egan and Wildman, 1992). Several trends make this possible, including the development of powerful new technologies, growing pressure to address social problems such as inadequacies in public education and rising health care costs, and a new appreciation among businesses, other organizations, and analysts of the role of information and communications in economic productivity (Egan and Wildman, 1992). The Internet demonstrates some of the possibilities: for example, there are a growing number of efforts (e.g., OncoLink from the University of Pennsylvania) to use the Internet as a kind of electronic "Patient's Desk Reference"—a source of hard to find or anecdotal information for people with rare or serious diseases such as cancer or amyotrophic lateral sclerosis (ALS)—or for self-help discussion (Bulkeley, 1995; Foderaro, 1995); there are the network pedophiles (among the first, it would appear, to exploit both the anonymity possible through electronically mediated conversations and the vulnerability of precocious adolescents); there are the first "experiments" with attempts to use the great efficiency of the information distribution capabilities of the Internet for advertising—and the first squeals of protest from those who (probably rightly) see a whole new world of electronic junk mail opening up; there is an Internet "radio station" broadcasting music from Santa Cruz, California, and beginning to strain the current limits of copyright law and performance; and there are merchants ranging from a small used clothing store in Los Gatos, California, with World Wide Web/Mosaic access through which customers can query a database regarding available stock, to Digital Equipment Corporation, which derived some $100 million worth of sales for a particular product line from publishing product literature and enabling benchmark testing over the Internet.[1]

Although many activities and products will not change, there will be new options in various arenas, and corresponding changes in market share for options on how to spend time as well as money. The frenzy of activity and "hype" noted in Chapter 1 points to the problem of differentiating a long-term vision from unrealistic promises of near-term products. The expectation for change in many quarters raises questions about what can be done as a nation and a people to learn from past mistakes with other media.

Discussion at the colloquium underscored a fundamental reality: while many executives and scholars recognize the potential for achieving social good, actual offerings of goods and services will depend on what sells, and perhaps as well on some broader vision of what is possible. While the profit motive is expected to promote multimedia programming for entertainment and various business applications, many colloquium participants emphasized the importance of developing other applications (e.g., for health and education). Their reasons were cultural, intellectual, and altruistic, and, in the context of debate over telecommunications policy reform, politically astute. By way of illustration, Richard Notebaert outlined a number of applications of telecommunications and information infrastructure to the improvement of health care. For example, the Wisconsin Health Information Network (WHIN) enables at least seven hospitals, over 250 doctors, and insurance companies to send and receive patient information electronically, through the public network.[2,3] While such experiences arouse interest in advancing the information infrastructure, the goal of maximizing benefits for health care, education, and libraries as well as more business-oriented domains raises practical questions of how to achieve sufficient scale, affordability, and interoperability.

Perhaps the most important theme of the colloquium discussions was the recognition by technologists, industrialists, and social scientists that there is no one way that digital convergence technologies and applications will or must develop. This variability is a principal reason that the social consequences of new media are among the most difficult of all effects to predict. Who, for example, would have predicted the emergence of "The Patriot Network" of the 1990s (Farley, 1994), which links ad hoc citizen militias, based on looking at the uses and users of networking as a preferred means of communication in the 1970s and 1980s? The existence of alternative paths for development of content and programming and for the mechanisms by which they are delivered will allow a variety of businesses to emerge and grow. Public policy, in turn, can affect the appeal of specific alternatives.

This chapter outlines some of the social issues raised by digital convergence. It focuses on issues where colloquium discussion clustered, including the enhanced flow of information, the shape that technology and applications may take, and the contrast between multiuser games and education as instances of the use of digital convergence technology. The chapter is intended to illuminate areas where choices by industry, consumers, and government will influence the benefits received from digital convergence.

THE FLOW OF INFORMATION

Even excluding entertainment, the proliferation of computing systems and their integration with communication systems has led many to predict that people will increasingly face a deluge of information. The human information processing system clearly is limited in capacity, leading many to wonder how growing information processing burdens will affect society. The social phenomena associated with TV and radio (e.g., the emergence of the "couch potato" in modern society) seem to signal a risk of potentially stupefying effects of sensory signal overload. The tighter integration of entertainment will compound that situation by providing more attractive packaging and delivery as well as more creative forms for that information. Eli Noam remarked that the challenge will be to sort through all the options. To date, he observed, computers generally have been used to produce new information rather than to manage it. He predicted that the technologies and business of systems integration will help process and reduce the glut of information. Others speculated about a need for wholesale rethinking of the business, public policy, and cultural aspects of information generation and management.

Most elaborate in his analysis was Richard Lanham, a professor of English at the University of California at Los Angeles, who called for a "new economics of human attention" (a somewhat different usage than customary in psychology). Information used to be more difficult to locate and assimilate in commonly available raw and often bulky formats, but no longer: technology is facilitating access to information. Today, the rarest fundamental resource is human attention, which gives information meaning and direction. Lanham's use of the word "economics" emphasizes the problem of allocation of attention as a scarce resource.

As the market for multimedia products develops, manufacturers must analyze human attention structures to learn what sells. Thus, the filmmaker and the literature professor who are skilled in getting attention, whether from viewers or students, assume central roles in the new economics. "What is converging is not only the technology of digital computation with the technology of mass entertainment. A larger conversion has occurred. . . . The arts barter the crucial economic good—attention," Lanham said, principally because digital-electronic expressive space differs from the printed page and analog-based icon and sound.

Lanham argued that it is time to rethink and reorient our approach to the information marketplace—in terms of both structure and social implications. "We have to bring the new economics of human attention to focus—now," Lanham advised. "We can't afford to study the problem to death." In defining the economics of human attention, Lanham outlined five fundamental differences between print and digital information:

1. Print, being fixed, is more authoritative than digital information, which is volatile, interactive, conversational.
2. The transition from print to pixel alters the text from a two-dimensional printed surface to a three-dimensional mixture of word, image, and sound, and thus requires a new mix of human attention skills.
3. These new skills introduce the process of modeling, with dramatic results. The viewer is encouraged to contemplate "what ifs."
4. The meaning of "originality" changes radically, with the result that current intellectual property law becomes obsolete. (This issue is discussed below in the section "Intellectual Property Issues.")
5. Finally, as ideas move into the rich space and sounds of digital expression, human motives change, with competition and play animating practical purpose in a fundamentally new way. This particular concept appears to emphasize the positive contributions that entertainment may bring to otherwise more serious endeavors. As discussed below in "Entertaining Education," however, achieving a net positive effect will not be automatic.

To benefit the most from digital convergence, society must acknowledge and respond to these transitions, Lanham warned. In education, for example, Lanham argued that the campaign to improve literacy is based on the old economics: no multimedia-based attention structure has yet been chosen to replace the traditional textbook, and there has been no accord on how to train librarians, or how to reconceive school "buildings" now that information is disembodied rather than fixed. Nevertheless, there are indicators that these conditions may be changing, however slowly (CSTB, 1994b). There is, for example, a substantial corpus of work developing on "constructive learning," which does begin to challenge the centrality of the hardbound textbook and does begin to explore and exploit new ways to "manage attention" through, for example, use of simulation and "construction environments." Experiments with electronic publishing and the elements of digital libraries may provide other examples.

Lanham identified two fundamental barriers to addressing such issues. The professional barrier, recognized by a number of colloquium participants in other contexts, is the rare and awkward nature of communication among the various disciplines involved. That challenge was noted by musicologist Robert Winter in commenting on his demonstration of multimedia music exploration applications: "I almost never do this in front of musicians. They're converted and they love it and they go do it. I preach to surgeons and physiologists and groups like this because what I'm addressing here and what Bob [Stein] showed you in his very exciting new projects are issues that are cross-platform, cross-discipline, cross-whatever."

The second obstacle is cultural. At one extreme is the camp that resists transforming the arts into commodities, while the opposing contingent seeks to maximize profits above all. "Just networking these two warring camps together is no solution," Lanham said. "Optical fiber, no more than twisted copper pairs, cannot heal a religious war."

Diversity of Information

Robert Stein of Voyager related the influence of profit-making strategy to the level of diversity in the information products delivered, building on his status as a publisher in both entertainment and education as well as on his personal philosophy. He said multimedia software appears to be developing along two tracks, the movie model and the book model, with the former prevailing. That is, Hollywood movie companies and game companies, and some traditional publishers, are focusing on expensive, large-scale productions—equivalent to movies costing tens of millions of dollars to produce. As a result, the number of U.S. films produced is limited;[4] the figure has been consistent at about 300 a year, Wildman has written (Wildman and Siwek, 1988). By contrast, approximately 150,000 new book titles are published in the United States each year,[5] thereby ensuring diversity in the marketplace.

"It is extremely important in society to have this breadth and diversity of material," Stein said. "Wouldn't it be a shame if there were only dozens of new things produced in new media and that was how our entire culture was being distributed . . . as a society, I'm not sure it's in our long-term interests to focus only on the blockbusters where you can make the money. I think you also have to have some diversity of thought. . . ." Compounding the need for diversity is the greater ability to exploit aftermarket opportunities, as discussed in Chapter 2, afforded by digital convergence technology. The impact of any one idea may be amplified by the ubiquitous, attention-commanding power of recursive delivery systems: the movie is the television show is the video game is the magazine is the cereal box is the talk of the schoolyard and the office.

True or full diversity of information is not necessarily an unmitigated good. Some observers have warned that, if the medium is the message, then advanced technology is bound to undermine cultural values. Such a concern was implied by Janice Obuchowski, president of Freedom Technologies Inc., who noted that in simpler times the cultural message was clearer. "As we move into this distributed, interactive, somewhat under-surface, almost anarchic environment," she said, "we need to at least concern ourselves to some degree—without becoming hysterical—about the issues of our society and who will communicate the cultural center." Although that center may become obscured by the ability of emerging systems to deliver an ever widening menu of cultural inputs and outputs, that diversity and pluralism are also positive developments, as noted by Robert Johnson of Black Entertainment Television (BET) in a late-1994 interview. Johnson related the proliferation of programming options to the recognition that the audience need no longer be assumed to be in one place, or homogenous. Others put on the table the fact that greater flow of information in general implies greater (and qualitatively different) flow of information that some find undesirable.

Ethical questions concerning programming shadow all the new conduits and forms of delivery, some of which, like the electronic theater, naturally attract social pressure. Society finds itself moving unwillingly into an uncomfortable, open-ended, and confrontational discourse to define "pornography" in media and calibrate damage to the young, the psychologically unstable, and the economically vulnerable.[6,7] In the same interview, Johnson observed that while a rough consensus may exist on the inappropriateness of pornography for children, it does not for other material that might be considered undesirable by some because of its political or hate-mongering character.[8]

The potency of pornography, violence (Kolbert, 1994), and gambling demand that mechanisms be developed to satisfy the ever-changing parameters of social values and government regulation, Alexander Singer has said.[9] Indeed, there is a skeleton at the feast of the entertainment industry's success, because its most profitable segment is the "action" genre, usually a euphemism for violence/ sadism. Also chafing to get into the starting gate is the $30 billion gaming industry (including lotteries, off-track betting, and local bingo games).[10] With its deeply addictive overtones and its appeal to vulnerable populations, this industry is not likely to enhance the reputation of interactive services, although it may enhance profits.

Singer has warned that if the private sector is unable to regulate itself then political and social extremists will impose rules from outside (Harmon, 1993; Jensen, 1994; Lippman, 1993). Singer has predicted that the complicated questions posed by new technologies will lead to the emergence of professional specialists in communications ethics. Recent announcements about voluntary standardization and labeling by the video game industry illustrate the kind of self-regulation that is possible, especially when the threat of government regulation appears imminent to an industry.[11] The telephone industry has also responded with mechanisms to control access to certain 900-number services.

Esther Dyson of EDventure Holdings Inc. commented in a late-1994 interview on the interplay between private ground rules and individual choice:

> Private organizations have a strong role in creating and managing environments where there are rules. People can decide for themselves which kind of environment they prefer, and go into those, as long as there are competing sets of rules where people can go. One of the nice things about cyberspace is that you can easily pick your environment. In the physical world, if you don't happen to like where you're living, it's hard to move. It's expensive, and there may not be room where you want to go. But in the Internet world, it's fairly cheap to change your environment, and I think it's very important that the government allow different outfits to set up places with different rules and then people can just decide where they want to go. . . . There should be some way to keep kids out [of inappropriate environments]. But I hope that's going to be more the job of the parents than of the government.

Singer emphasized at the colloquium that, regardless of attempts at control, the market will be flooded with information products of questionable value. This phenomenon will not spell the extinction of artistic merit, but it will exploit business opportunities and consumer demands. The existence of demand for digital pornography is already well in evidence.[12] Noting that pornography was the driving force behind VHS videocassette technology, Singer said the sheer volume and diversity of new products may obscure the quality work. "None of those groups will control anything," he said. "This is not a controllable phenomenon. You will get a tidal wave of garbage, of excitement, education, penetrating intelligence and appalling degeneracy. Count on it . . . . It is appropriate, I think, for regulatory agencies to have certain limits on obscenity, privacy, and so on. All of that seems well advised, but you cannot stop the flood of junk . . . ."

Intellectual Property Issues

The supply of information available will reflect a variety of environmental factors and incentives, which relate to risks, rights, and responsibilities for buyers, sellers, and others (CSTB, 1994c). The most identifiable and at the same time most controversial area of incentives is that of intellectual property protection.[13] Intellectual property rights command special attention because the content dimension of digital convergence consists of intellectual property.[14] The discussion below highlights some of the issues; a comprehensive assessment is beyond the scope of this report. The issue of intellectual property elements in associated technical standards is noted in Chapter 2.

As many have observed (CSTB, 1994c), digital technology effectively invites piracy: audio, video, and textual material can be copied perfectly, easily, and inexpensively. Broadcast networks, for example, have begun to face the problem of finding images to which they own rights (e.g., from programs that they own) rebroadcast over the Internet, where they are accessed for viewing and other uses on personal computers.[15] This situation is one of many that raise questions about how rights owners will be able to track down or even find out about infringers. Some suggest that it may be time for a new model of intellectual property rights that takes into account these changing conditions; others observe that copyright, introduced for printing, has been successfully adapted for cameras, radios, player pianos, and so on and will adapt yet again.

Multimedia introduces unique problems into the copyright arena, because its various components have different legal traditions. For example, the book publishing industry relies on comprehensive contracts, while the movie industry frequently employs short "deal" memos, and the computer industry has little experience with copyright issues such as "performance rights" (Radcliffe, 1993). Whereas the movie industry typically asks for compensation up front, the music industry has traditionally sought royalties based on performances. Compounding these differences among producers of multimedia materiel is the new control afforded the customer: the number of times something is performed, displayed, or distributed is up to the user, and therefore hard for the producer to measure or estimate in advance. For example, new video-on-demand systems that allow viewers to watch a program any time of the day could involve thousands of "broadcasts" a day of a given program (Chartrand, 1994). Such patterns are driving media industries (e.g., publishing, TV/video, movie, music, and software) to explore new approaches to collecting money for use of their intellectual property, including various kinds of blanket payments in lieu of paying at each instance of use.

A related issue pertains to enforcement and administration. For example, the distribution of songs through databases offered by such commercial providers as CompuServe has raised questions about who is liable for copyright infringement: the person who provides a copy of the copyrighted material may clearly be infringing, yet the owner of the database may be much easier to target (Woo, 1993). Case law is beginning to define or refine expectations, although the possibility of legislative reform remains.

The very nature of interactive media—its malleability—can make it difficult to pinpoint the original "author" or even the confines of a "work" itself. As one expert in the field has observed, "In a certain way, the distinction between the author and user of material becomes blurred, if not obsolete. Therefore, in the not-too-distant future, there might hardly be any more authors, but a multiplicity of 'contributors.'"[16]

A fundamental issue is the interplay of creativity, communication or sharing, and compensation. This was illustrated by Singer, who recounted the networking experience of the Writer's Guild of America (WGA), an association of scriptwriters. WGA members developed a network for conversing and exchanging ideas. According to Singer, the network fostered "witty, bright, and rich interchange between some hundreds of people who were rather isolated and need one another's support." But after a year and a half, uproar over alleged theft of ideas led to the dissolution of the network, Singer said.

A new arena in which existing law may be tested is that of fine art. Computer and software companies are negotiating with museums around the world for rights to scan images of famous photographs or paintings for distribution of copies via CD-ROM or electronic networks. Technology allows both high-resolution image storage and display plus copying via printing by users. To date, a typical arrangement has been a nonexclusive license to reproduce the high-quality photographs museums make for other purposes (Hudson, 1995).

U.S. copyright law was strained even before the digital revolution. In practical experience, originality involves borrowing elements of the past, blending memory, repetition, chance, and invention in a new mixture, Lanham said, offering insights based on his own experience as an expert witness in some 50 copyright violation cases. By contrast, copyright law is based on the premise that there can be absolute originality. "In this view, the 'original' is the poet, alone in the garret, coming up with something absolutely new and, of course, redemptive for mankind. The history of copyright law in America has been a series of attempts to adjust this exaggeration to how originality actually works in human life. The new space of digital expression now forces us to make this adjustment in *theory* as well as in practice," he said.

Copyright law could constrain multimedia development, Lanham warned. He identified three problems that need to be resolved.

The first problem is how to define "substantial similarity" of visual images. That is, if a generative code can create images, and those images can change in an interactive environment, then what is being compared to what? When this issue arose in a case involving an Apple Computer user interface, the judge invoked an even stronger standard of "virtually identical," which is even more difficult to meet for images, such as computer-screen desk-top representations, that change all of the time as a function of their use. Increasingly, that dynamism is characteristic of user interfaces as well as multimedia titles.

The second problem is structural. Multimedia technology, by enabling the reader to rearrange, rewrite, and link text in a nonlinear manner, has eliminated the fixed concepts of beginning, middle, and end, which traditionally have been the principal points of comparison between two works. Third, any discrimination between idea and expression is impossible when a digital code can generate music and images, Lanham said.

"What emerges, for better or worse, from the multimedia environment as it has operated on young people and as I think it is going to operate in the future, is really a redefinition of human reason," Lanham asserted. "It's a redefinition of the nature of propositional thought. . . . If that changes, then the whole nature of the relationship of expert testimony, for example, to how a jury thinks about the ordinary common reader, common viewer, common listener experience—and how they judge a case—is going to change."

In the information age, the law of real property may become secondary to the law of intellectual property, Lanham suggested. Inasmuch as digitization broadens and increases the volume of information access, there may need to be a rethinking of whom rights owners really want to protect against. Thus, for example, according to Lanham it may be appropriate to establish two levels of intellectual property, one for software professionals and another for amateurs that extends the principle of fair use (i.e., a copying that is not an infringement). Given scholarly traditions regarding proper citation and crediting correct sources of ideas and other inputs, questions arise about prospects for greater flexibility and acceptability in situations that involve "borrowing," say, of pieces of film or text for student projects. The act of borrowing is becoming easier; the context, constraints, and culture are therefore becoming stressed.

The debate over compensation for intellectual property revolves around the fundamental premise of intellectual property protection: that compensation induces production, and that therefore intellectual property issues must be addressed if new information technologies are to be developed fully. As suggested above, interesting and vexing intellectual property issues are associated with multimedia "material" other than content or interactive titles, such as the multimedia interfaces of computing or other digital information systems. In the area of computer interfaces, courts have *weakened* laws over the past few years. Can copyright and patent laws be evolved to protect what in many cases are vastly expensive research and development investments in, for example, human interface design? These issues are actively being contested in courts today—if the "look and feel" of a human-computer interface cannot be protected by current copyright statutes, as many have argued, will it be possible to protect multimedia content or interactive "titles"? Or is content easier to produce than interfaces, suggesting a different set of issues?

The intellectual property conundrum is compounded when the issue of patents is added in, although patents have received less attention in this context than copyright (because of the volume of activity involving some form of publishing or expression of ideas, which is the domain of copyright). However, a few controversial patent cases illustrate the potential for small businesses to substantially influence industry directions as well as costs. For example, in 1989 Compton's New Media, a division of the Tribune Company, applied for a patent relating to indexing functions that could apply to both CD-ROM and on-line services, described as the "multimedia search system using a plurality of entry path means which indicate interrelatedness of information." A patent was awarded in August 1993 and announced, together with Compton's intentions to collect royalties, in November 1993 at a major trade show, Comdex/Fall (Lewis, 1993b). The legitimacy of the claim was reevaluated by the U.S. Patent and Trademark Office (PTO), and the patent was disallowed shortly before the 1994 session of Comdex (Chartrand, 1994). Another recent patent case involved data compression technology, affecting a variety of software and electronic communications and resulting in a settlement combined with equity interests between the parties, Microsoft and Stac. A recent change in PTO hiring policies to increase the computer science-related skill level in its work force is a step in the right direction. So is PTO's own moves to exploit information technology by creating a digital library of patent information.

THE SHAPE OF TECHNOLOGY

Precisely how new information technologies will change American culture remains a matter of conjecture, but also a matter of choices to be made by many parties. Noam observed that, historically, analysts have been overly optimistic about the short-term impacts of technology but have underestimated the long-term effects, such as the extent to which the automobile or the television has changed how people live, work, and interact. Stein, who questioned whether, in hindsight, the automobile in its present form was a positive invention, emphasized the need for a long-range vision in technology development. He acknowledged that,

> No doubt technology is going to get better and stronger and we'll find lots of uses for it, but fundamentally, it comes down to where we want to go. These are questions which I think particularly this society, the American society, is not very good at asking. We don't usually ask ourselves where, as a society, do we want to be—which machine do we want to build, and for what purpose? . . . [E]specially because we've had so much experience now with technology in the 20th century, it's the question that, it seems to me, we could start to ask ourselves. What is the long-term meaning—not just in terms of next year's profits, but the long-term in terms of decades and centuries—of the machines that we're going to build? I don't believe for a minute that machines are neutral.

Colloquium participants suggested that intelligent management of new information technologies is the key to maximizing their benefits. This view was most optimistically advanced by George Gilder:

> I think the technology is enormously beneficial . . . I don't think there is any significant downside. I think that technology is what we are as human beings. We create new tools. That's how we emerge from the muck. This is the adventure of our lives and our culture. To pretend that it's somehow an optional or negative force is to deny the very essence of human beings. I just think that it's a positive force that has to be intelligently managed, but it's entirely positive.

> It's particularly an egalitarian force. These technologies are getting cheaper and cheaper, and they will be most beneficial for poor people, who currently suffer most from our school system, for example. These technologies really will allow any person [in any neighborhood] to take instruction from the best professors on the face of the Earth, or to walk through the halls of the Louvre with close examinations of the paintings. The world opens through this door
> . . . .

By contrast, Donald Norman of Apple Computer Inc. cautioned about overly optimistic predictions:

> The history of technology shows that every successful technology has been successful in directions that were not forecast by the people at the time. . . . The fax machine was invented in 1870 and it still has not made major inroads into the homes. Technologies have to meld themselves into the fabric of society, but if we're not careful, it'll lead us in ways that we don't want. You can't control what really happens, but we might be able to prevent the negative from happening and that's my message for today.

Noam remarked on the complex interplay of technology, behavior, and institutions or norms:

> The notion that somehow everything will be the same except that you now have a more convenient way of getting to Joe Smith is simply unrealistic. We'll have to develop protocols of who can talk to whom and when. Then, the sense of community is going to radically change because again, we have certain constants. If it's much easier to talk to some people with whom it was more difficult to talk in the past, it means that something has to give. Certain forms of communications atrophy as other forms of communications become cheaper and more convenient. The sense of community changes and you begin to develop electronic communities—telecommunities—[raising] all kinds of interesting political issues.

Stein remarked on how difficult it can be to predict the full impact, including benefits, of entertainment-related technology by observing that while the placing of a person on the moon had been long anticipated, one of the significant aspects of that milestone was not predicted: that it would be televised, allowing hundreds of millions of people to watch it together. Stein noted that from the 1930s through World War II, machines were portrayed in educational films as liberating people, whereas advertisements in the 1950s paired housewives and domestic machines.

While Gilder appeared to assume relatively steady demand for bandwidth in terms of the applications he mentioned, Stein emphasized that the adequacy of available bandwidth depends on who the users are, and by extension, the kinds of uses and therefore the kind of bandwidth needed per communications channel.

> If you think about sending video out the way it is sent out now, there is plenty of bandwidth. But if you think about the possibility of everybody on Earth communicating with everybody else, and high resolution with moving pictures and sound, under George's definition of what is enough bandwidth, there probably isn't enough bandwidth. I don't doubt that humanity will solve the problem and we'll eventually have more bandwidth, but I think the question is, What kind of society do you see? Do you see a society where a small group of people is talking to everybody, or do you see one where everybody is talking to everybody else?

Stein's comments underscore the challenges of achieving scale and universal access in supplying new services and the associated questions about who controls what. The benefits Gilder described, for example, are attainable once fiber is deployed—but the high cost of that deployment, combined with investors' needs to reap returns on that investment, suggests that considerable cost barriers remain to redeploying moderate bandwidth.

Stein contrasted the big investments associated with things like game technology with a paucity of investment that supports good thinking. "I would love to see somebody think about making a machine whose goal was to present a program that encouraged people to think about something—to reflect and also to communicate with other people who are thinking about these things." Explained Stein, "I'm obsessed with two things. One is getting people to think. The other is getting them to think with each other." Stein suggested that, given the different kinds of computing and communications systems already being developed, some kind of hybrid system to achieve his vision is technically feasible—but technology alone is not sufficient. "The problem is it's probably not a machine that anybody wants to buy in terms of it's not a productivity tool, a game machine, but it's something our society probably needs desperately."

One reason that such a machine seems elusive may be the divergence in cultures and approaches of the industries that might have to combine to make it work. As Norman noted, technologists focus on producing technology while the entertainment industry focuses on producing content. "I would imagine what we need is what Singer and Stein were arguing for, which is some attention to the content . . . what our media are about and not simply the technology that links people, but perhaps in a mindless way." A full convergence remains to be achieved.

The Need for User-Friendly Technology

A call to action was submitted by Norman, who said it is more important today than ever before to develop "humane" technology that takes into account user needs and capabilities. The current approach to technology development, Norman said, has barely evolved since the 1933 Chicago World's Fair, for which the motto was "Science finds, industry applies, man conforms."

The technology-centered approach requires users to operate in ways not consistent with their natural or learned predispositions; often the human behaves in "appropriate ways"—it is the *technology* that does not! This mismatch results in a high proportion of industrial accidents caused by human error, making occupational safety and health a motivation for progress in human-machine and human-computer interaction. A more human-centered approach could reduce human error, decrease training time, increase acceptance of technology, and bolster U.S. competitiveness, Norman said. Although the United States leads the world in research, development, and application of human-centered design principles, especially in industries such as personal computers, the lead is tenuous, and most industries still rely on extensive training to reduce errors.

"This is a critical issue as we move toward a fully interconnected, fully communicating world in which the social and organizational issues will be as important as the technological ones," Norman said. Part of what is required, observed Nancy Stover in a late-1994 interview, is reducing the emphasis on how technology works. This is essential to making the technologies of digital convergences less intimidating. A sign that a technology has succeeded, according to Stover, is a focus on its benefits; how many of us know or need to know how the telephone works?

Singer suggested[17] that added complications arise in connection with decisions that are, at a fundamental level, aesthetic. What appear to be primarily technology choices profoundly affect the most powerful existing communications medium—the picture. He went on to observe that the consequence of what will be a significantly more compelling image could have broad social and economic ramifications. For example: What would be the impact on local economies if the huge increases likely in TV "catalogue" sales (via the shopping channels) seriously displaced conventional retail sales income?

Information processing will alter video consumption options, according to Steven Wildman. "As we add more channels, what we're changing is the logic of the consumption of the video product," he said. "If we change that logic, then the nature of the assistance provided to consumers or programmers by the industry itself changes as well." Although opportunities for greater user or audience control and format choices are expanding, it is likely that consumers will continue to receive, in the traditional manner, the well-established and well-received forms of passive entertainment that now exist. As BET's Johnson noted, when people use a television, they do not expect to ask it to retrieve or analyze data.

Johnson speculated that computer-based technology may permit a return to traditional behaviors:

> It used to be [that] you'd sit around a campfire, or the living room, and someone would start telling a story. And if you didn't understand something, you could say, "Wait, tell me about when the knight came upon the dragon, what happened?" And you could ask, "Dragon? How big was this dragon?" You could interact, and get the information you wanted. Well, it's only since television came along that you can't stop, and you can't ask somebody to explain what happened because the film is running, or the tape is running. Interactivity is something that has been a part of our information access for a long time.

The introduction of the remote control device increased viewer control over video consumption, but providers still "nurture" the consumer to some extent, Wildman said. For example, cable operators prefer to position their channels near a broadcast network, to increase the likelihood of attracting viewers who "surf" the channels. But the market will respond with new techniques for searching across channels, Wildman said. He suggested two possible paths: programming services offering a preselected menu of different types of shows (i.e., prepackaged video magazines), and set-top converters or "intelligent" television sets, which would help viewers make their own selections of programs and services. In a variation on the latter concept, the cable television industry is developing interactive program guides that viewers will be able to operate using a remote control device (NCTA, 1993c). Interactive program guide work at CableLabs will enable consumers to search for programs by time of day, channel, and theme, and facilitate selection for taping. The StarSight program guide technology, drawing on broadcast control codes, is being licensed to TV and VCR makers as well as satellite and cable TV operators (Fleischmann, 1995). In a late-1994 interview, Robert Lucky cautioned that the design of program selection technology will affect its impact:

> Even if all content providers have equal access to a telephone line, if the person that builds the interface to your set-top box is making it difficult for you to choose someone's programming, you're not going to ever get there. And there's going to be such a plethora of material that the way you're gently steered, one way or another, is going to make all the difference in the world. This is something even more than a technical problem. It's going to be a problem for ethics and culture to truly make this open. Actually it will be very difficult.

Although too new to receive much attention at the colloquium, the explosive growth of the World Wide Web and its Mosaic interface suggest a computer network variant of the user selection concept, one that has even spawned business ventures aimed at helping individuals and businesses to use the Web (Churbuck, 1994). The contrasts between the Internet and emerging television-based interactive environments underscore that "interactive" and "two-way" may be matters of degree. Argued Stein in a late-1994 interview,

> The thing about the Internet is that it isn't two-way communication, it's every-way communication. That's where the big struggle is going to be, to maintain that kind of environment, because we're going to have very different kinds of programming if we maintain every-way communication than if we go to simple two-way communication.

Other speakers stressed that technology should be related to context. Stein noted that, in Pacific Telesis' conceptual video of life in the year 2005, advanced technology was in wide use but apparently had not improved the *quality* of life: the neighborhood was run down, workers suffered job stress, and student skills and parent-child relationships were poor. "There is no sense that people's actual experience has changed at all . . . the reality is, unless we are conscious of the kind of society we are building, the machines are not going to make equality for us. They never will," Stein declared.

Stein's comments underscore the importance of making improvement of the quality of life an explicit objective in introducing new technology. But they beg the question, Whose objective should that be? Stein, an entrepreneur, acknowledged that businesses competing in the information marketplace focus on objectives supporting the quest for profit and growth, raising yet other questions about the role of government and other players.

A History Lesson:
The Evolution of Books as Mass Media

In an ideal world, technology would be available on an equitable basis to all. One model for achieving universal access is the distribution system for print media. This infrastructure includes a taxpayer-supported system of postal carriers and roads for the physical movement of publications, as well as public libraries. The far-reaching system has provided for a richness and diversity of print resources, encompassing a wide range of perspectives and unfiltered sources of information.[18]

Whatever the possibilities of an idealized future, Paul David warned against overlooking near-term realities. The issue is not the technology itself, David said, but the need to develop and apply it by acting within social organizations, to address problems of trying to mobilize resources, especially other people's money and talent, for the uncertain and unproven.

And the difficulties don't end there, David said. "When all the foregoing daunting challenges have been met, and when the innovations and questions are perceived by others to be potentially competitive with and, therefore, disruptive of their established interests—as all important innovations turn out to be in some respect or other—then there may ensue the life-and-death struggle against seeing the whole venture aborted by hostile takeovers, or crippling regulatory restraints, or outright suppression of its use by political authority."

As an example of tortured evolution of technology, David recounted the history of the book as a platform. It is a tale of long delays, significant technical advances in multiple fields, and strategic intervention by authorities.

Movable type was invented around 1440. But initially the Gutenberg revolution transformed the reading habits of only elite European society, not the masses. It took more than two centuries for the first popular novel—*Pamela*, by Samuel Richardson (1740)—to be printed, ushering in the era of books as mass media, David said.

There were difficulties concerning standards, concepts, and layout, and the book's ultimate form was shaped by its development under a set of monopoly privileges that had nothing to do with authorship, but rather protected an industry that was unstable because of high first-copy costs, David said. Predictably, the monopolists focused on the luxury market, packaging books with bindings and other expensive attributes. "In that sense, they delayed the development as a mass medium, which could have been developed at an earlier stage using graphics," David said. "Graphics was available, and there was a market for it. Cheap books were available, too, but the market structure . . . that existed pushed it in a different direction."

The evolution of printing hinged on technical progress in various trades; these advances set the stage for eventual exploitation of the small market that had created the culture of the manuscript book. Developments in the linen industry provided an inexpensive paper medium, and advances in optics made reading glasses possible for the far-sighted. The practice of metallurgy was affected as well, because Gutenberg's invention essentially signaled a breakthrough in foundry work and processes, David said.

Finally, the Venetian aristocracy promoted development of the printed book by underwriting and financing the work, coping with related political problems, and using books for government publications. "They developed the book to govern what was Venice's growing empire, as an aid in that as well as in pursuit of a set of humanistic values which were embodied in the culture of the book," David said.

USING THE TECHNOLOGY

The nature of the content and the delivery system will evolve more or less together, in the context of the ways in which they are used. Games and education capture two ends of the spectrum and yet are increasingly discussed as elements of common applications.

Games, Play, and Life

The growth in the popularity and profitability of electronic games has inspired interest from many quarters. Indeed, cable industry moguls John Malone and Ted Turner have speculated publicly that games may be an ideal vehicle for encouraging consumers otherwise accustomed to passive television watching to become more interactive users of TV (Lippman, 1993). A variety of entrepreneurs have begun to find business opportunities in the new means and mechanisms for play, providing striking echoes to the scholarly description by Huizinga (1950):

> Summing up the formal characteristics of play, we might call it a free activity standing quite consciously outside "ordinary" life as being "not serious," but at the same time absorbing the player intensely and utterly. It is an activity connected with no material interest, and no profit can be gained by it. It proceeds within its own proper boundaries of time and space according to fixed rules and in an orderly manner. It promotes the formation of social groupings which tend to surround themselves with secrecy and to stress their difference from the common world by disguise or other means. (p. 13)

Interactive games and services delivered over computer and other networks expand the potential beyond that offered by stand-alone game platforms. Advanced information technologies allow individuals who have never met, who are separated by thousands of miles, to get to know each other. For example, many students use the Internet to participate in Multi-User Domains (MUDs), virtual communities that were designed initially as sophisticated role-playing games. Since the first MUD program was written in 1980,[19] several hundred similar games have been developed based on various concepts, such as the television program *Star Trek: The Next Generation.* Researchers and scientists also are becoming interested in these communities.

As identity workshops for issues related to control and mastery, MUDs can serve a therapeutic purpose, according to Sherry Turkle, who called the phenomenon a "deadly serious" game world, "precisely because they are not simple escapes from the real to the unreal, but because they're betwixt and between, they're both in and not in real life." Turkle has argued that a computer is like a Rorschach test[20] in allowing for projections of the self, but that the computer goes even further than a standard psychological test because it is part of daily life. Extending this metaphor, virtual communities not only enter into daily life, but can also *become* daily life, because unlike conventional games, they do not have an end-point. Explained Turkle:

> The boundaries are more fuzzy. The routine of playing them becomes part of their player's real lives. Such blurring of the boundaries between role and self presents new opportunities to use the role to work on the self, and not the least of these is the opportunity to play an aspect of yourself that you embody as a separate self in the game space.

Thus, virtual communities extend the potential value of role-playing games by blurring the line between the game and the real world, she said.

In the *Star Trek* MUD, more than 1,000 players spend up to 80 hours a week engaging in intergalactic exploration, creating new roles for themselves, and interacting with others. A player explained the attraction of the game to Turkle:

> You can be whoever you want to be, you can completely redefine yourself if you want. You can be the opposite sex. You can be more talkative. You can be less talkative, whatever. You can just be whoever you want really, whoever you have the capacity to be. You don't have to worry about the slots other people put you into as much. It's easier to change the way people perceive you because all they have is what you show them. They don't look at your body and make assumptions. They don't hear your accent and make assumptions. All they see is your words . . . .

The situation is a little more complex, since through grammar and diction words can be quite revealing, yet there is evidence that at least among school children the desire to present the best appearance to one's peers can promote greater attention to writing skills (CSTB, 1994b).

The MUD experience has transformed Peter, an isolated physics graduate student whose life revolves around his work, Turkle said. Peter never has traveled. MUDs offer him an opportunity to interact with people, travel, and create an ideal self. "His favorite MUD is actually located on a computer in Germany. He calls this travel. It's from MUDs that Peter has learned what he knows of politics, economics, and the differences between capitalism and welfare state socialism . . . the room [space] he inhabits on the MUD is elegant, romantic, out of a Ralph Lauren advertisement. Beyond expanding his social reach, MUDs have brought Peter the only intimacy and romance he has ever known."

In a larger cultural context, such role playing provokes examination of not only individual identity, but also cultural identity. Using MUDs, Turkle said, ". . . people are exploring, constructing, and reconstructing their identities. They are rethinking social issues about gender, about privacy, about property, and about what constitutes legitimate authority in a community."

The MUDs, their parallels in computer group gaming, and virtual reality technologies doubtless provide a unique and invaluable laboratory for social psychologists. This utility comes at a price, however. Unlike the withdrawal into the interior, reflective world of the book, the new environments vastly amplify their effects. As systems become more refined, complex, and compelling, their explorers enter terra incognita. Some of the less stable pioneers may become addicted or, as biologists say, "lost to the gene pool" (O'Neill, 1995). Indeed, one incident that generated media and cyberspace attention involved the suicide of a young man who immersed himself in electronic network environments, environments that close observers maintained had sustained rather than alienated him.[21] More recently, attention flowed to a situation in which network users were able to mobilize assistance from afar to avert a suicide (Bowles, 1994).

Turkle underscored how rich the concept of digital games really is:

> Sometimes, this dismissive notion of "all they'll do is play games" [ignores the fact that these are] a very serious and, in many ways, very constructive kind of game. . . . [What] I'm describing is a mixture of the creation of text, the creation of literature, and programming. It really is the first best example that I've ever seen of [the] potential for an entertaining crossing of the two-culture divide. People who are working in these worlds need to create objects with the programming language and also create text as they work. Many of them are kids. They are learning by building objects—they're actually learning to construct and make things—which is the best way to learn. They're forming communities of people with whom they remain in contact, often breaking their anonymity and finding another setting. So, if you allow this revolution to reach people, they're going to do what kids enjoy: at this point, what gives people joy is communicating with other people.

The social dimension of interacting over a network and the combined entertainment and educational value of that interaction were recurring themes in late-1994 interviews with Esther Dyson, Stephen Case, Samuel Fuller, and David Nagel.

For example, Samuel Fuller of Digital Equipment Corporation commented on the value of

> a distributed learning environment where a group of a dozen people could work on a topic, maybe moderated by a teacher, but where the content that is flowing back comes from asking questions or responding to other questions, so that they as a group of a dozen people begin to learn about a topic.

In addition, the individual and group interactions that take place over networks have important secondary effects. Observed Nagel in another interview,

> You are seeing new cultures, new forms of journals or magazines, which are devoted to a growing, and I think an avant garde, subculture of people who spend a lot of time in what they refer to as cyberspace. It's becoming, in the same way that MTV did a few years ago, . . . a general understanding among the general population, even if they don't participate in it. . . . The idea that it's an important phenomenon is becoming part of the popular culture.

Entertaining Education

The potential benefits of interactive multimedia in education are perhaps obvious, and colloquium participants were poetic about the possibilities. Singer, who developed entertainment programming concepts for virtual reality, foresees breathtaking applications of this technology in education: "Imagine taking a trip through the brain, for example, for a group of surgical students. A brain the size of a cathedral, in the presence of a master surgeon or a master teacher . . . ." Such applications could be all the more stunning in an electronic theater, he has noted. Progress toward this vision is under way with release for access via the Internet of a three-dimensional, computer-generated body produced by the National Library of Medicine's Visible Human Project (RSNA, 1994). As Paul David said, just as the printing press has done, multimedia learning environments will "empower individuals, unlock worlds of knowledge, and forge a new community of ideas." See Box 3.1 on the benefits of interactive media. Publishers, news services, cable companies, software companies, and others have been experimenting with PC-based, on-line, and broadcast multimedia programming for education, with mixed success.

On a broader level, several participants emphasized the promise of long-distance learning, which could bring the best teachers and latest techniques to even the poorest districts. The telephone and cable industries are involved in interactive distance learning projects, as are various segments of the Internet environment (state and regional networks, supercomputer centers, universities, and so on).[22]

Notebaert pointed to Ameritech projects as illustrations of the potential. For example, the SuperSchool traveling demonstration model involves more than 30 applications for education available through the public telecommunications net-

---

Box 3.1 The Benefits of Interactive Multimedia

Some interactive products permit the type of reflection and experimentation that Donald Norman describes. A successful purveyor of this approach is the Voyager Company, which has published electronic books, plays, and music on CD-ROM and movies on optical video disk. Managing partner Robert Stein focuses on the "experience that is developed for the reader or user in conjunction with the author," rather than on the nature of the medium.

Interactive multimedia offers a number of advantages over conventional media, according to Stein:

• It allows the user to *experience* history. Voyager's CD-ROM version of a U.S. history book adds approximately 5,000 original documents to the basic text, along with audio, video, and animated graphics. History books are essentially a filter of the author's analysis of original documents, Stein said, whereas CD-ROM provides for a dialogue with the author and "allows the reader to become much more of a participant in the process of history." Of course, CD-ROM does not eliminate biases.

• It can further understanding of cinematic history. Voyager's optical disk version of the Beatles' movie *A Hard Day's Night* contains added material such as film outtakes, script excerpts, background information on songs, and profiles of the cast and crew.

• It can attract a new audience to an old art form. Voyager's interactive version of *Macbeth* allows the user to play a chosen character's role, a karaoke feature that could make Shakespeare's play come alive for reluctant readers. Similarly, a CD companion to Beethoven's Symphony No. 9 allows music students to experience and learn by "browsing" through the composition, repeating sections as desired and calling up information about particular instruments.

---

work, including distance learning classes between the United States and the Montreal World Trade Center, a user-controlled weather laboratory featuring a thunderstorm simulation, a computer-simulated voyage through the human body, and a homework hotline.[23] Another project, ThinkLink, connects the classrooms of 115 Michigan fourth-graders to their home television sets via fiber-optic cables.[24] Ameritech has an agreement with the school district to procure programming, schedule it, and package it; local teachers select the programs, such as a drama series on solving math problems (Ameritech, 1993a).[25] Observed Notebaert, "It's hard for me to accept the fact that children go to school today in a 19th-century classroom and then go home to Music Television (MTV), which I think is far more entertaining and educational, although on the wrong end."

Expanding on that concern, Donald Norman, a cognitive scientist who is an Apple Fellow, warned that the MTV model is not entirely appropriate for education, in that television programming and advertisements are divided into very small segments so as to retain viewers' attention. "The experiential mode of thinking that this creates, I think, is the opposite of the reflective mode, which is what is required for new thoughts. What I am afraid of, as we merge these industries, is that this fun and enjoyment of the experiential mode might tend to dominate and take over from the reflective mode," he said. The ease with which multimedia can incorporate recreation and fun into educational material is well established, but that capability may not be an unequivocal benefit. Educational applications should be longer term and deeper in substance than entertainment applications.

"MTV is a good model for the entertainment industry, but school isn't meant to be entertaining; it's meant to be educational, profound, and deep," Norman said. "It's meant to allow people to reflect and to experiment." BET's Johnson pointed out that "edutainment" is not new—there were occasional instances in 1950s and 1960s television programming—but that the new media are fostering more of this kind of programming. Norman explained that what is at issue is how capabilities presented by new technologies are selected and used:

> This is not really a statement for or against technology. This is a statement about the ease of doing something with one technology that may drive out other things. We know that we can create technologies that lead to reflection and we saw a wonderful example at the prior lunch demonstrations. Robert Winter's demonstration of a music program, which allows you to reflect, to compare, to play this segment of music and play that segment of music and go back and forth and compare and contrast them, and to count the rhythms and watch the score and to read an analysis is a kind of reflective medium that comes out of that technology. What I'm trying to argue for is that when we develop our technologies, we worry a lot about what they make possible, whether it is easy to do and whether it is hard to do. What I'm afraid of is that we will be too easily driven to a machine-centered view and to this experiential view.

Several speakers argued that, if distance learning is to be successful, entirely new approaches must be developed. Notebaert explained that new media drive the need for new approaches: "We are currently working with Indiana University in teaching distance learning in Indiana. The professors that are doing the course development, the curriculum, have had to go back to school using what the entertainment industry already knows and redefine the content and the methodology for delivering the content in this different medium." This teaching method can have a remarkable effect, he said. "Each student is then able to interact at his or her own pace and own speed, so those kids that normally would have been called hyperactive, all of a sudden we find being different individuals," he said. Similar explorations are being applied to adult education and (re)training.[26]

Another factor creating a need for new networks may be the increasing emphasis on visual material. In a late-1994 interview, Janice Obuchowski explained,

> People are reacting much more to the visual than to the textual. You see that in the declining readership of newspapers. That is very much a generational thing . . . . In fact, I've heard it said that video has become the language of the home.

That's going to present a real challenge to teachers. They're going to need to communicate more visually. At the same time, they're going to have to persuade their students that there's still some value in something other than that more right-brained visual response. To make it in a highly competitive world economy, you have to be analytical, you have to be literate, you have to be numerate and some of that doesn't get learned just visually.

Despite the emergence of the technical capabilities, however, it is not clear whether they will necessarily resolve the motivational issues that underlie reflection and learning—and that drive the markets for the goods and services that embody these capabilities. Educational experts have noted, for example, that the supply of good software and other content matériel for computer- and communications-based education remains limited—there are lots of products, but the quality is often disappointing. Moreover, the relatively limited penetration of personal computers into both homes and schools and the difficulties experienced by educators in incorporating computer- and communications-based technologies into schools underscore the fact that a range of financial, cultural, programmatic, administrative, and technical hurdles must be overcome for these technologies to achieve the potential envisioned by Gilder and others (CSTB, 1994b). As Johnson observed, the profit remains in the business market, which serves sophisticated customers willing and able to pay for new technologies; the pace of implementation in education will continue to be slow, reflecting the existing technology base and limited availability of funds.

Winter of UCLA, who developed the Beethoven CD with Stein, was enthusiastic about the new technology, asserting that, while education is indeed a matter for "serious, profound, and deeply appropriate" work, it is also true that children learn by having fun. The traditional method of teaching novices to read music is about as captivating as giving a beginning swimmer "a lecture on fluid dynamics," Winter said.

Winter's goal is to attract new customers, "people who absolutely hated high culture, who hated Beethoven. . . . I think this technology, in a sense, is a way of getting new customers for whatever you're doing . . . . We're hearing Beethoven or Stravinsky or Dvorak or anybody's music in ways they couldn't hear it."

NOTES

1. Samuel Fuller, Digital Equipment Corporation, late-1994 interview, characterizing a late-1993 new product line launch.

2. A doctor can fill out a generic insurance form, for example, which the software translates into the particular form required by the patient's insurance company. The system is expected to improve patient care and to reduce paperwork generation and administrative training needs. Administrative costs have been reduced by over 19 percent, according to Notebaert. Information concerning WHIN was drawn from Notebaert's presentation at the colloquium as well as Ameritech (1993b,d).

3. The cable television industry also is involved in the health care arena. For instance, nursing students and faculty members in Idaho can watch live surgery under way at a local clinic on a cable system originally designed to broadcast college basketball games; the students also can ask questions of the operating team. See NCTA (1993b).

4. Approximately 800 hours of cinema production compare to some 8,000 hours of television production in Hollywood (Flaherty, 1993).

5. Reed Reference Publishing, New Providence, New Jersey, personal communication, November 8, 1993.

6. Some research has provided examples of TV-linked increases in violence (Kristol, 1994).

7. This concern must be considered within the current context of extreme intergenerational conflict. While it always has been true that the primary injunction for younger generations seems to be to agitate and defy the establishment, contemporary variations on this theme suddenly make the game meaner-spirited (imagine interactive "gangster rap") and oddly disquieting. The cacophony not only has turned nasty but also suggests a questioning of values hardly seen since the years of the flower children and the Vietnam War. For instance, a popular rap song encourages murder of the police; a syndicated cartoon show, *Beavis and Butthead*, has incited mimetic behavior resulting in suicidal arson and delivers its enormously popular message in a form seemingly "dumbed down" to witlessness; and within a two-week period the three major television networks broadcast competing versions of the same murderous teen-aged sexpot's "real life" story. The principal changes in moral values and particularly in pop culture across the last half century may be less fundamental than the result of a confluence of symbiotic phenomena. These phenomena are readily identifiable. Also consider the very real cultural chasm between age groups. The propensity of successively younger age cohorts to live increasingly in electronic environments accentuates the erosion of cross contact between age groups: 12-year-olds cannot make contact with 16-year-olds, who have little in common with 20-year-olds. Clearly, the familiar 25-year generation separation is splintering into shortened cycles of generational change, reflecting the shortened cycle of technology development. Older forms of expression are beleaguered and seem ill-suited to the times. The discourse sometimes seems to be in an unfamiliar tongue, given the profound impending cognitive change in the way humans think about and use language (see Lanham, 1993).

8. See Schwartz (1993); CSTB (1994c).

9. The material in this and the next paragraph was drawn from Alexander Singer, personal communications, February 1994.

10. In March 1995 St. Martin (Caribbean)-based Internet Casinos Inc. announced plans to launch a casino accessible through the World Wide Web by mid-1995 (*IISR,* 1995).

11. Video game cartridges will be rated by the Interactive Digital Software Association, and PC software and CD-ROM games will be rated by the Software Publishers Association (Farhi, 1994).

12. At the major computer trade show Comdex in 1993, hundreds of new software titles were on display, moving beyond early generation of reference books to include children's games and X-rated items. "One Japanese computer dealer, who asked that his name not be used, said it appears that pornography may be the long-awaited 'killer' application that will spur the sale of CD-ROM drives" (Lewis, 1993a).

"'In the privacy of their own home, people will try things and do things that they would never be caught dead going to an adult bookstore for,' said Howard Rheingold, author of *Virtual Community*" (Garreau, 1993). Interactive entertainment over a network has unique properties: "Computer sex has obvious similarities to 900-number phone sex, not to mention magazine sex. But this new medium is also quite different. After all, these are real people finding each other in cyberspace, not a paying customer calling a professional."

13. There are several legal issues associated with the evolving national information infrastructure (NII), such as privacy, security, free speech, and intellectual property rights. Considerable attention was paid to these issues in 1994, through the administration's Information Infrastructure Task Force and its Information Policy Committee and through congressional hearings.

14. Disney, for example, is noted as recognizing the value of its copyrights for creative content as a critical asset, one giving it relatively high levels of flexibility; see Turner and King (1993).

15. Personal communication with Minna Taylor, Fox Broadcasting Company, October 10, 1994.

16. See Dreier (1993); Dreier is department head at the Max Planck Institute for Foreign and International Patent, Copyright and Competition Law in Munich.

17. Alex Singer, personal communications, February 1994.

18. This analogy is drawn from Kapor (1993).

19. A brief history of MUDs can be found in Kelly and Rheingold (1993).

20. The Rorschach test, named for Swiss psychiatrist Hermann Rorschach, is a personality and intelligence test in which a subject interprets inkblots.

21. "[Nathaniel Davenport's father] eventually understood how some people have found something so compelling in this on-line computer world that they have all but pulled up stakes and moved into cyberspace, paying little attention to what most of the rest of us think of as real life. And in the end, Davenport came to believe three things: That computers did not kill his son. That he had not known his son. And that his son had been a bold and gifted pioneer in something exciting and creative and scary and cool, a still-furtive revolution in art and expression . . ." (Schwartz, 1994).

22. An extensive listing of cable projects, including those related to the "Cable in the Classroom" initiative, may be found in NCTA (1993c).

23. The applications have been used by students in Washington, D.C., and the Great Lakes region (Ameritech, 1992, 1993f).

24. The system is based on the "video dial-tone" concept. A switch in the neighborhood telephone center feeds signals between the homes and the two schools; televisions and computers are connected to data sources by high-speed telephone lines. The system includes a set-top box and special remote control unit and "mouse" pointing device.

25. Sixty-seven percent of the homes accessed the ThinkLink system at least 20 times during a two-week sample period; parents indicated the material not only has enhanced their child's learning but also has allowed them to be more involved. See Ameritech (1993a,d) and Lashinsky (1993).

26. In work settings, electronic training systems involve virtualizing tasks with intensive use of simulation, and providing just-in-time knowledge and learning systems (including groupware) to front-line workers (Perelman, 1993).

4

Promoting Competitiveness:
Policy Issues and Obstacles

Digital convergence introduces new problems into the ongoing debates over international competitiveness, telecommunications policy reform, and the evolution of the information infrastructure. Policymakers are challenged to balance the different priorities, national interests, and legal and regulatory traditions of the telecommunications, computer, and entertainment industries. At the same time, there is pressure on government to act—both to relax existing laws and rules and to enact new ones—because information technologies are evolving more rapidly than ever before.

Central to the policy debate are the prospects for an enhanced information infrastructure, which galvanized private- and public-sector attention during 1993-1994.[1] Legislative efforts during that period constituted the first major attempt since passage of the Communications Act of 1934 to alter the goals and frameworks for state and federal regulation and the constraints on business entry by common carriers provided by the Communications Act of 1934 and the Modified Final Judgment codifying the breakup of AT&T.[2] Although telecommunications reform legislation failed to pass in 1994, new legislation was introduced in 1995. Contention about the specifics suggests that whatever legislation does pass will launch a process in which various parties will seek to fix and fine-tune those aspects that affect them.[3]

Developments over the ensuing months indicate that comments at the colloquium were symptomatic of the kinds of concerns being expressed in multiple forums. They reflect the political process that has driven legislative efforts to overhaul the legal and regulatory framework for telecommunications. For example, Samuel Ginn, speaking then as the head of a regulated common carrier

(Pacific Telesis), was perhaps the most forceful in criticizing the constraints on telecommunications firms, contending that "public policy and regulatory policies will be the most significant factor in determining whether these kinds of services can be made available to the public, not technology." Ginn asserted that public policy and regulation will be the most important factor—and one of the toughest challenges—in making advanced information services available to all. Similarly, Ameritech's Richard Notebaert said government policy is the "major speed bump" inhibiting the application of technology to solve societal ills. Beneath these general statements lie concerns about the mechanisms (e.g., delays and uncertainties associated with multiyear proceedings) as well as the objects (e.g., ability to enter certain markets, terms of participation in certain markets, and pricing constraints) of regulation. Those concerns were aired universally in a series of late-1994 interviews (Appendix C lists those interviewed), suggesting that between 1993 and 1995 both interest in market entry and concern about constraints had grown among the various players in the digital convergence arena.

Despite concerns about the impact of regulation on the cost and profitability of a given investment, comments by several participants suggest a broad recognition that absent government intervention, the owners of key capabilities control timing and access. Thus Ginn observed, "It's not clear to me, given the way the markets are developing, that there is an opportunity here to serve all elements of society unless you have intervention in terms of social policy."

The proliferation of public interest advocacy groups in the 1993-1994 period attests to a broadening concern about how the public policy agenda for information infrastructure is being set and how various objectives are weighted when decisions are made. Yet another face on this concern was provided by the change in the Congress with the 1994 elections. This process of politicization also reflects a recognition that the distribution of benefits from digital convergence will vary over time: costs come down and access can broaden over the long term. The question raised by public interest advocates is, How long will and should be the wait for mass access to technology's benefits? The question emphasized by business is, Who pays to direct or accelerate receipt of benefits that do not derive directly and naturally from the evolution of various markets?

INTERNATIONAL COMPETITIVENESS

Because of leadership in the fundamental markets associated with it, digital convergence, in the judgment of the colloquium steering committee and other observers, should contribute significantly to the economy and international competitiveness of the United States. U.S. companies lead the world in most aspects of computing and communications technology and entertainment programming; in addition, innovation-stimulating market competition is more prevalent in the United States than in rival nations, and English increasingly is becoming the international language of commerce and entertainment (Memmott and Maney,

1993). David Nagel asserted that, despite recent erosion of U.S. dominance in computers, "it's clear still that nearly all of the interesting innovations, both in computing and in telecommunications, are being driven in the U.S. industrial base." Whether this dominance is sustainable, Nagel said, depends on whether U.S. firms have learned the lessons of the past and can apply and profit from their own innovations.

Entertainment adds a new and unknown variable to the mix: it is seen as a source of economic benefit to its purveyors, but unlike computing and communications tends not to be seen as an "intermediate good" or vehicle to broader benefit except as an item of mass consumption. There are therefore more assumptions than facts when it comes to assessing entertainment's contributions to competitiveness. In a late-1994 interview, Peter Cowhey, formerly a professor of international relations and political science at the University of California at San Diego, noted that entertainment products are receiving more attention in trade policy, with leaders in some countries showing growing concern about the prevalence and impact of U.S.-originated programming. It may require explicit action, he suggests, to point out and ensure that the expanding, advancing global information infrastructure will provide capacity for distributing cultural outputs from everyone—it is not an exclusive vehicle for distributing U.S. content, although global distribution outlets (of which Music Television may be a crude forerunner) are likely to emerge, and it broadens the market for cultural outputs generally (i.e., it makes the pie larger).

A sister issue, notes Cowhey, is the issue of ownership of media. Current U.S. policy restricts foreign ownership of broadcast media to 25 percent,[4] and some countries are introducing reciprocal restrictions or program quotas to limit U.S. entry, in particular.

The National Telecommunications and Information Administration (NTIA) also warned in a 1993 report that the United States "cannot afford to be complacent about the success of U.S. media firms in international markets. Recent regulatory and technological changes require U.S. policy makers to continue to adapt in order to promote the development of international mass media markets that are open and competitive—the type of markets in which U.S. firms historically prosper" (NTIA, 1993). The NTIA made a series of recommendations designed to foster economic growth in the mass media industry, not only in the United States but also—because of the global nature of the industry—worldwide.

The United States has provided fertile ground for development and application of a number of services that provide a working foundation—in the form of corporate learning and consumer familiarity and expectations—for digital convergence. As Michael Borrus has argued, technical progress depends on an economy's potential for "learning by doing and by using" (Borrus, 1993). See Box 4.1. Use of digital technologies has not only benefited organizations and individuals within the United States, but has also provided the basis for the development of global enterprise, including global service industries that tap and

---

Box 4.1 Contributions of Business-oriented Network-based Services

Several successful, highly profitable on-line services (legal, financial, and medical) serve professionals and specific industries (e.g., computerized reservation systems (CRSs) in air transport). CRSs have dramatically improved the efficiency, speed, and effectiveness with which travel agents can make and change reservations, and they have improved load and resource management for the airlines. They are also increasingly accessible to individual consumers for direct reservation transactions.

800-number services now generate about $10 billion per year for telecommunications companies; they constitute a major portion of long-distance telephone network traffic during certain hours, are profitable, and are growing. Almost everyone uses them to make reservations, to order merchandise, and to contact the customer service organizations of providers of goods and services. 900-number services, which tend to be more entertainment-oriented, are also a large and profitable business, as are automated voice response systems.

All of these information systems are enabled by the convergence of computers and communications, and sometimes entertainment as well: the customized call-processing in 800-number service is enabled by complex computer systems; interactive voice response systems (for inquiries about an account, to change investment options in a 401(k) account, to issue a buy or sell order for securities, and so on) involve consumer use of touch-tone pads to communicate upward to a server, which communicates downward with synthetic speech. Although these systems use a different set of multiple media, they are completely analogous to using a keyboard on a terminal to communicate upward, and the display on the terminal to communicate downward from the server. The apparently large and growing economic impact of these on-line services provides a basis for expecting growth in other services combining various computer- and communications-based media.

---

deliver knowledge and talent wherever it resides or is needed (CSTB, 1992, 1994a). This phenomenon has itself resulted in a refocusing of trade policy and trade negotiations on trade in and conditions for service industries as opposed to physical product or commodity distribution. Cowhey remarked on these developments in a late-1994 interview:

Digital technology made it possible to start thinking about global service enterprises. . . . A bank in Cleveland can be a bank in Tokyo. So the digital revolution allowed services to imagine themselves to be global enterprises, and now the trade negotiators are starting to say that means we have to integrate and liberalize these markets and bring them together. A second great revolution is that trade negotiators are now tackling the problem of foreign investment rights, and starting to bring some notion of what are minimum rights of foreign investment. And in turn that means that these high-technology enterprises start to be able to define the fact that yes, I can go to my customers, and yes, I can find a way of bringing my technologies to bear in your market by being on the ground and seeing what people need.

Cowhey noted that the large and diverse installed computing base has led to an artificially large U.S. lead in digital convergence.[5] He observed that it is reasonable to expect greater diffusion—and associated benefits—of personal computers and other systems in at least the industrial nations. Moreover, explained Fuller in another interview, "By its very nature, an information utility or an internetwork will be global as well as national in scale, and issues of geography will become less important." As Cowhey noted, the 1993-1994 public statements of President Clinton and Vice President Gore focused attention on information infrastructure across the industrialized world, making it folly to assume that only the United States would place emphasis in that area. Indeed, the "G7" industrial countries held their first ministerial summit devoted to a single industry when the European Union hosted the February 1995 "G7 Ministerial Conference on the Information Society." The European Union particularly championed the event in order to build political support for European regulatory reforms necessary to catch up with the United States. Box 4.2 lists 11 multinational pilot projects agreed upon at the G7 summit, which also resulted in agreement on several high-level principles:[6]

- Promoting fair competition;
- Encouraging private investment;
- Defining an adaptable regulatory framework; and
- Providing open access to networks while
- Ensuring universal provision of and access to services;
- Promoting equality of opportunity to the citizen;
- Promoting diversity of content, including cultural and linguistic diversity; and
- Recognizing the necessity of worldwide cooperation with particular attention to less developed countries.

European nations have recently moved to launch their own video-on-demand trials, often drawing on U.S. technology. The cable television business is more advanced in the United States than elsewhere: U.S. firms are supplying cable equipment and programming worldwide. Further, as George Gilder observed, "No other country in the world has broadband connections to 60 percent of homes or passing 90 percent of its homes." Although there have been publicized instances of high-level capabilities in specific locations overseas, the actual average capability available to almost all households appears higher in the United States than elsewhere. On the other hand, foreign suppliers of consumer and other electronics, such as Thomson Consumer Electronics, are a significant presence in the U.S. market. Although slower European progress has been attributed to the high cost of installing high-bandwidth communications facilities, advances in data compression and other technologies for more fully exploiting copper wire and advances in computer systems have been cited as encouraging European

Box 4.2 G7 Project Matrix

Theme Area	Main Project Objective
Global inventory	To create and provide an electronically accessible multimedia inventory of information regarding major national and international projects and studies relevant to the promotion and the development of the global information society. An assessment of social, economic, and cultural factors impacting on its development will also be undertaken.
Global interoperability for broadband networks	To facilitate the establishment of international links between the various high-speed networks and testbeds supporting advanced applications.
Cross-cultural education and training	To provide innovative approaches to language learning, in particular for students and for small and medium enterprises.
Electronic libraries	To constitute from existing digitization programs a large distributed virtual collection of the knowledge of mankind, available to the public via networks. This includes a clear perspective toward the establishment of a global electronic library network that interconnects local electronic libraries.
Electronic museums and galleries	To accelerate the multimedia digitization of collections and to ensure their accessibility to the public and as a learning resource for schools and universities.
Environment and natural resources management	To increase the electronic linkage and integration of distributed databases of information relevant to the environment.

efforts. Moreover, cellular telephony has spread relatively rapidly in Europe, aided in part by agreement on a supporting standard (GSM).

Tempering the discussion of competitive advantage and disadvantage, Borrus suggested that evolving international business relationships may become more complex and cooperative. He noted that the United States controls the "soft" side of the electronics industry—from design, architecture, and marketing to software and systems integration—but that key hardware technology and manufacturing activities have been migrating to Asia. "No one geographic region, and certainly no individual company, has all of the necessary know-how to develop this next generation of electronic systems," Borrus said. Yet the persistence of U.S. leadership in software and U.S. reliance on offshore manufacturing raise questions

Global emergency management	To encourage the development of a global management information network to enhance the management of emergency response situations, risks, and knowledge.
Global health care applications	To demonstrate the potential of "telematics" technologies in the field of telemedicine in the fight against major health scourges; to promote joint approaches to issues such as the use of data cards, standards, and other enabling mechanisms.
Government on-line	To exchange examples of experience and "best practice" in the use of on-line information technology by administrations in establishing procedures for conducting electronic administrative business between governments, companies, and citizens.
Global marketplace for small and medium enterprises	To contribute to the development of an environment for open and nondiscriminatory exchange of information and to demonstrate the interoperability of electronic and information cooperation and trading services on a global scale for the benefit of small and medium enterprises.
Maritime Information Systems	To integrate and enhance environmental protection and industrial competitiveness for all maritime activities by means of information and communication technologies, including applications in the area of safety and the environment, intelligent manufacturing, and logistics networks.

SOURCE: Matrix reproduced from a document found on the World Wide Web at http://www.ispo.cec.be (EC Information Society Project Office Webserver) under *G7 Information Society Conference* category and *Key Documents* subcategory.

about what trends and indicators are most reliable. Moreover, it may be that digital convergence represents an opportunity to reclaim areas lost to foreign competitors, such as consumer electronics, to the extent that such areas become more computer-like.

Eli Noam has said that international asymmetries hamper the global system of systems, which will function effectively only if it is competitive at each stage, and if regulation establishes nondiscrimination. At present, the information infrastructure stands at uneven levels of development in technology and policy across the globe; most countries still have an established monopoly communications provider, and outside of the United States monopoly remains the dominant communications paradigm. Government policies and limited competition abroad may be a greater impediment than available technology; certainly, those factors have limited both deployment and experimentation with computing and communications technologies in the past, to a far greater extent than have policies in the United States. Telecommunications reform is emerging in many countries (Hudson, 1994; Lavin, 1995), and considerable discussion has surfaced over the desirability of more market-oriented regimes (Bangemann et al., 1994).

In a late-1994 interview, Cowhey seemed to anticipate the 1995 "G7 Ministerial Conference on the Information Society" by describing the importance of policy relating to broad social objectives as a factor in the international competitiveness dynamic:

> Now Europe, for example, has been very strong in emphasizing public service through the digital technologies, but they've been weaker on benefiting from competition, and they're trying to change their mix today. And if the Europeans get the mix right and we don't, then they may become the model for the rest of the world. . . . The United States has to show that this digital revolution does speak to larger concerns about making schools work, making hospitals work, and making it possible for people to share in the benefits of information technology, not just in New York, and Washington, D.C., and London, and Tokyo, but also in the many poorer countries of the world.

Borrus also pointed to the need to address international asymmetries in technology access. He has warned that the U.S. supply base is likely to be more accessible to foreign rivals than is the Japanese market, and that software skills and technology can be appropriated more easily than can manufacturing components and expertise (Borrus, 1993). Borrus outlined the problem of how to assure equitable access to both U.S. and foreign companies. It is easy to invest in a U.S. company and thereby gain access to know-how,[7] but very difficult to gain similar access to a Japanese company, for example. The Japanese have discriminatory public procurement policies (COC, 1993), and their *keiretsu* system of business alliances establishes preferential sales, supply, and capital allocation arrangements that impede market access by new entrants.[8] Also, there are far fewer publicly held companies in Japan (2,000 as of 1987) than in the United States (24,000; Gerlach, 1992). Borrus anticipated a shift in U.S. trade policy to deal with the access problem. Experiences in the semiconductor arena illustrate the possibilities; see Box 4.3. In pursuing open markets worldwide as a trade policy objective, suggests Cowhey, the United States must attend to concerns in other countries that they not open their markets at a point in time when the United States appears to be closing its own.

Another, more perplexing problem, according to Borrus, is to identify the foreign technologies and know-how that should reside in the United States, and to find ways of moving them here. An example is flat panel displays, used in applications such as laptop computers. Flat panel displays were invented in the United States over 35 years ago, but Japanese companies now control over 95 percent of the burgeoning $3.5 billion market and outspend U.S. firms on display

---

Box 4.3 Semiconductors and Trade Policy

The United States relies on foreign suppliers for some computer hardware components, such as dynamic random-access memory (DRAM) computer chips.* The semiconductor chip was invented some 30 years ago in the United States, but in the mid-1980s Japan gained a majority share of the global semiconductor market, and U.S. companies were virtually eliminated from the critical DRAM market due to Japan's system of industrial organization and its dumping (below-cost sales) of chips in the U.S. market (COC, 1993; Cowhey and Aronson, 1993). In the U.S.-Japan Semiconductor Arrangement of 1986 (renewed in 1991), Japan pledged to prevent dumping, to help U.S suppliers gain access to its markets, and that U.S. firms would have 20 percent of the Japanese chip market by 1991. In addition, the U.S. government and industry cooperated to form the research consortium SEMATECH. Both of these approaches have had some success, and by the end of 1992 the United States had regained its leadership in the global semiconductor market, and Japanese firms were moving some of their production overseas (COC, 1993; Cowhey and Aronson, 1993).

---

*See Borrus (1993) for an accounting of gaps in the U.S. technology supply architecture for components and U.S. dependence on foreign semiconductor equipment and materials.

---

research by more than 20 to 1. Various means have been explored for strengthening the U.S. base in display technologies. "Dumping" duties were imposed on imported Japanese displays in 1991, but that trade policy has had mixed results. The Advanced Research Projects Agency launched a research initiative to promote innovation. A broader approach may be called for. However, the Republican congressional leadership has expressed strong doubts about such programs, worrying that they constitute little more than subsidies for large electronics firms.

Symmetrical international access to technology—including increased U.S. access to certain technologies—will not emerge unaided. There is no unanimity on the precise mix of policy. For example, Gilder has criticized the semiconductor agreement praised by Borrus. But Borrus captured the terms of the policy discussion when he wrote that trading blocs need "(1) to agree on a set of principles that endorse reciprocal access to regional markets, investment opportunities, and supply base technologies; (2) to negotiate for tangible results that mitigate the disruptive impacts of domestic practices that violate agreed norms of behavior; and (3) to develop new multilateral institutions for coordinating bilateral regional moves" (Borrus, 1993).

Cowhey has noted that trade pacts have limited effect, in part because so much of world commerce is now determined by investment flows and global production strategies of multinational firms. This has heightened the importance of emerging industrial alliances in international competition. For example, IBM Corporation has established a joint factory with Japan's Toshiba using the latter's liquid crystal display technology, and the two companies are working with Siemens of Germany to develop an advanced (256-megabit) dynamic random-access memory (DRAM) chip (Cowhey and Aronson, 1993). Of particular significance is the location of development teams at IBM's facilities in New York State. Such alliances permit the development of common, global infrastructures for technology development and allow firms to reduce the costs and risks of producing extensive product lines, Cowhey has noted (Cowhey and Aronson, 1993). National technology and trade policies, especially those for the information infrastructure, have to be evaluated in light of their impact on these alliances because much of the world's information infrastructure will be developed by such alliances.

How to design policies to stimulate innovation and promote competitiveness remains a subject of contention. A Council on Competitiveness project recently concluded that, if policymakers determine that U.S. development of a certain technology is in the national interest, "then they must create an integrated, systematic approach to the industry which includes capital market reform, the establishment of consortia, [and] support for the underlying technology infrastructure, along with trade policy" (COC, 1993). That report argues that policies to stimulate technological innovation in the United States are a necessary complement to trade policy.

Unfortunately, achieving an integrated, systematic approach is elusive. Experience in economics and industry suggests that chaos and conflicting efforts do better. The high-definition television (HDTV) situation, subject to a variety of interpretations, is a case in point. See Box 4.4.

One area where there appears to be consensus on the need for government action is international aspects of intellectual property protection, a source of growing concern as the information infrastructure becomes more global. The federal government has recognized the need for stronger intellectual property laws worldwide and in recent years has promoted international standards in this area. For example, the United States joined the Berne Convention for the Protection of Literary and Artistic Works[9] and has bargained with other countries through the General Agreement on Tariffs and Trade and other regional and bilateral negotiations. Since digital transmissions are increasingly global, and since our evolving national information infrastructure is effectively part of a global information infrastructure, some mechanisms will be needed to handle the problem of differences among countries as to what constitutes a copyright infringement. For example, the concept of a parody as a fair use does not exist in all countries.

Box 4.4 High-definition Television: A Case Study

The United States was a late entry in the high-definition television (HDTV) arena. Research on HDTV was initiated in the 1960s in Japan, where the first HDTV transmissions and prime-time programming were offered (COC, 1993). Even in the late 1980s, the conventional wisdom was that an analog HDTV standard would be pursued, until General Instrument Corporation demonstrated the potential for a digital approach (General Instrument unveiled the first all-digital system in 1990). That development encouraged constructive engagement by the Federal Communications Commission (FCC),* which established an industry-led and industry-funded advisory committee to evaluate competing HDTV standards (COC, 1993). The Japanese standard was disadvantaged by the FCC's decision to try to get HDTV into 6-MHz channels to make it easier for the established broadcasters, earlier lukewarm toward HDTV, to play.

The FCC's standards advisory committee began evaluating HDTV systems in 1991; in 1993, Japan's system, acknowledged as inferior to the digital systems, was pulled from the competition, and the European Community indicated that it probably would adopt the U.S standard (COC, 1993). The three remaining electronics teams in the contest announced they would collaborate to produce a standard system (COC, 1993).

The saga of HDTV illustrates that government action may be perceived in different ways. The Program on Digital Open High Resolution Systems at the Massachusetts Institute of Technology has outlined two views of HDTV standards development.** The industry view is that the government refrained from either subsidizing or designing HDTV technology, acting merely as an arbitrator in industrial development. The alternate view is that the innovative U.S. proposals derive from a government-industry partnership, in which agencies such as the Department of Defense*** support academic and other private research on underlying technologies, such as image compression, high-speed computing, communications, encryption, flat panel displays, and viewer requirements. Relatively small U.S. governmental research investments in fundamental computing and communications technologies have had large payoffs in the form of U.S. industry and competitive advantage (CSTB, 1995).

---

*For example, the FCC established the standards evaluation group, required that HDTV transmissions be compatible with existing television systems, and developed a timetable for the selection of a standard (without allocating new spectrum, thereby motivating video compression research). Such actions stimulated the private sector to attain world leadership in underlying technologies, such as digital transmission (COC, 1993).

**"America's Approach to HDTV: a Government-Industry Success Story," a paper prepared in May 1993 by the MIT Program on Digital Open High Resolution Systems (DOHRS) for Rep. George Brown (D-CA), then chair of the House Space, Science, and Technology Committee.

***Over a four-year period, the [Defense] Advanced Research Projects Agency funded close to $300 million in research and development of high-resolution video display, digital signal processing, and data compression technologies (COC, 1993).

PUBLIC-PRIVATE TENSIONS AND
THE INFORMATION INFRASTRUCTURE

The tension between cultivating an integrated approach and leveraging the unexpected fruits of competition and some degree of market chaos is epitomized by policy debates relating to the evolving information infrastructure.

An overview of the U.S. approach to managing digital convergence was provided by Cowhey. The forces driving the domestic market are the pursuit of profit, political opportunity, long-standing industrial and technological structures, and cultural values, he said.

> Essentially, the American bet has been to ride the back of the rise of distributed intelligence and processing power, to break apart the traditional hierarchical telecommunications networks, to distribute computing power, and to open up new types of software avenues.

> That, in turn, led to a regulatory policy emphasis upon rewarding new entrants in the market as a policy priority, emphasizing cost cutting—not just simply because lower costs and lower prices are nice, but because it encourages growing use of the communications network. Because use is sensitive to price, lower prices have encouraged users to experiment with new ways to use new information services [and] new ways of getting interaction among these competing computer and communications technologies. Much of the most important innovation comes from users, not producers, and this has proven a major competitive advantage for the United States.

> Regulatory policy has also emphasized the idea that we'll accept fragmentation among the different pieces of the industry, although today we're all trying to talk to each other across these market segments. What we have to recognize is that one of the curses of America's experimentation is that fragmentation of the industrial structure makes it very hard to get technical cooperation in a pooling of efforts.

But foreign rivals have their own difficulties, Cowhey said. Europeans have encouraged technical cooperation among producers to achieve early integration of knowledge and effort. They have discouraged new entrants in the market and have not encouraged price cutting. The growth of interactive information industries is constrained by the slow changes in pricing and service practices of the telephone companies, and hardware development is sluggish because networks are providing the wrong types of incentives. Japan, meanwhile, has introduced some competition into its telecommunications industry, but the new telecommunications carriers are owned by equipment suppliers and, to some extent, by their large corporate customers. Moreover, public policy still tilts toward subsidizing equipment suppliers at the expense of users. And regulators have not allowed the dominant telephone companies to get into cable television.[10] But even this barrier may fall, as Bell Atlantic Corporation's progress in pursuing judicial and regulatory authorization to offer commercial video programming over its telephone distribution system attests (Landler, 1995; Carnevale, 1994).

"We're living through a great moment of experimentation here, and part of our problem in making public policy is that it's not self-evident which bet is right," Cowhey said. Both the European Union and Japan decided in 1994 that their approaches had to change. The European Union required the introduction of competition in voice telephone services by 1998. Japan reformulated many regulations that had hindered competition and actively debated breaking up NTT, its dominant phone company.

The United States also wrestled with changes in 1995. It was trying once again to legislate permission to allow the regional Bell operating companies, cable systems, and long-distance carriers to enter each other's markets. It also promised (in a speech by Vice President Gore at the 1995 summit of the G7) to remove the 25 percent limit on foreign ownership of spectrum, a limit that the foreign firms cited as a bar on their market access to the United States. The Vice President promised to achieve this goal by either legislation or regulation by the end of 1995. The one condition was that restrictions on foreign investment would be removed only for countries that liberalize their own markets. In short, this was an offer to liberalize on a bilateral basis with like-minded countries.

The same speech by the Vice President affirmed an even more sweeping goal, that is, success in the General Agreement on Trade in Services (GATS) trade negotiations on liberalizing basic (i.e., voice) telecommunications services scheduled to conclude by April 1996. If successful the GATS pact would make true competition in telecommunications services into a binding trade obligation for major industrial and some developing countries. Such a pact was considered unthinkable even 10 years ago.

The promise of information infrastructure clearly depends on considerable investment by private parties. At issue are not only competing technological and business approaches, but also the degree to which facilities and services offered by different parties can interoperate. Technical features—including those relating to openness and symmetry in communications, equity in access to infrastructure, and who gets to enter what markets—are among the key issues that informed colloquium discussions and more recent debates. These features have figured in the development of regulatory reform legislation, and they are also at the heart of initiatives relating to standard setting for voice, video, data, and multimedia services as well as to the formatting and transfer of various kinds of information and documents. For example, the Cable Act of 1992 provided for measures to foster greater compatibility between consumer electronic devices and cable television systems, resulting in digital convergence-related standard setting by the Federal Communications Commission (FCC) and industry. Also, the administration sponsored a mid-1994 workshop to identify key issues and options for facilitating standards development. But it is an open question as to how far the government can or should go in promoting the kinds of standards needed for digital convergence; its efforts are likely to focus on points at which different networks and other infrastructure come together.

PERSPECTIVES ON REGULATION

Colloquium participants suggested that government policies with respect to digital convergence should be guided by two general principles: first, that relaxation of traditional forms of regulation and increased market competition are beneficial in general; and, second, that there will continue to be a need for government intervention, but in different forms and areas than in the past. For example, many referred to growing (perceived) needs to protect intellectual property rights and to ensure that those who control a conduit not have a monopoly on the content that goes through it. Behind such comments lies the recognition that a growing portion of the investment in and returns on information infrastructure relate to information or content. Although most of the policy discussion reflected conditions in the telecommunications industry in particular (and within that the telephony component), many comments were relevant to information industries in general. On the other hand, there is little foundation in terms of regulation and other legal constraints affecting entertainment technology, and possibly even less constraining the computing industry.

The first principle may be obvious, because the benefits of market competition are well known. Noam and Cowhey have documented, in separate papers (Noam, 1995), the benefits derived specifically from the breakup of AT&T. Noam, in an analysis of the accuracy of various predictions concerning deregulation, has concluded that the doomsayers generally were wrong—that few benefits attributed to the monopoly system were lost. He found that proponents of deregulation were right more often than were pro-regulators, although liberalization evoked new issues that have been addressed effectively by regulation. In addition, Noam has concluded that the telecommunications sector is more dynamic and innovative as a result of deregulation.

Cowhey also has pointed to the benefits of liberalization, citing a number of statistics: since the breakup of AT&T, long-distance service cost has declined about 50 percent, the average household has seen a reduction in service costs, and the productivity of telephone companies has climbed an estimated 40 percent, all while these companies have introduced greater innovation in services and increased flexibility for users (Cowhey, 1990).

The second principle—concerning the changes in policy needs—requires thorough exploration. The breakup of telecommunications monopolies and the emergence of new media are having two primary effects on the policy-making landscape, Noam explained. First, there is less need for regulation to balance the power of small users facing giant, often monopolistic suppliers. Second, price and quality regulation also becomes less important as a systems integration industry emerges and begins to compete for consumers.[11]

According to Noam, government should not react to this transformation by picking favorites—that is, by influencing or impeding change to favor any particular technology or carrier. Expanded Robert Johnson in a late-1994 interview, even the best-intended government intervention can distort the market, interfering with market demand and entrepreneurial creativity. Noam and others generally agreed that policymakers may need to promote rules of the road for the "network of networks," such as in interconnection and common carriage. Policymakers need to assure access to scarce facilities that could become "bottlenecks" in the marketplace, and they need to address international access asymmetries, he said.

As noted earlier in this report, with the development of specialized networks and the evolving need for content-selection aids, the economics of basic carriage become less attractive. The real advantage to a network owner increasingly will accrue from diversity in programming and services, and so there will be expanded opportunities for niche marketing; a network owner will become, in effect, a manager of a shopping mall, housing many "boutiques."[12]

In their quest to enter new markets, telephone companies have contended that substantial traffic must be generated to justify the building of fiber networks, that voice alone will not generate such volume. The NTIA, in a 1993 report, maintained that freeing telephone companies to provide cable programming would stimulate competition in the video market and provide incentives for infrastructure development, and, furthermore, any resulting increased demand for video programming could stimulate international trade (NTIA, 1993). Wildman has argued that, given the substantial costs of desired network upgrades and the nation's dependence on private investment to cover them, policy restrictions on the business opportunities of information providers should be reduced.[13] This is the essence of the arguments advanced by telephone companies, although companies differ in their preferences for what restrictions are most critical to relax.[14] Foreshadowing if not encouraging recent legislative and rulemaking debates, the NTIA had recommended relaxing restrictions on networks owning cable systems,[15] common ownership of television stations and cable systems in the same market,[16] national multiple ownership,[17] and foreign ownership. Its own interests affected, the cable television industry contends that restrictions on cross-ownership should be relaxed only if the Congress acts to repeal state laws barring cable companies from providing telephone service.[18]

Greater freedom for telephone companies may involve unbundling or providing other service providers more direct access to basic network facilities and service elements. To that end, some have submitted proposals to the FCC and state regulatory authorities for unbundling their networks.[19] The theory behind these proposals is that, by giving up their monopolies, regional telephone companies become deserving of entry into other markets, such as long-distance services. However, the technology of open data networking makes unbundling both easier to achieve and economically more compelling than it has been, although most telephone companies may continue to resist ceding the control and revenue streams historically associated with bundled service provision (CSTB, 1994b). That is, the nature of the new technologies threatens to make traditional approaches to assessing infrastructure investments obsolete.

Noted Noam, "Private carriers are now increasingly competing with common carriers, and conversely, common carriers will increase and compete with what private carriers do today. Those [situations] require all kinds of new forms of legal arrangements for dealing with traditional problems." Noam elaborated on the underlying economics:

> . . . when [common and private contract carriers correctly] compete head to head, one has to serve everybody indiscriminately in similar classes of customers at similar rates and the other one doesn't. The one that has more flexibility has an inherent advantage with all other things being equal. You can price people differently and, therefore, undercut for some customers, depending on their price elasticity. You can undercut the one that has to provide the same price for everybody, particularly when you cannot prevent arbitrage. Where one cannot prevent arbitrage, but the other one can, you cannot, even if you wanted to, have price discrimination because of the arbitrage issue. Similarly, if one has access rights to the other, but the other doesn't have access rights to the first, then you have asymmetries of the kind that whenever a transmission segment on the common carrier is cheaper, the private carrier will use it. If it's the other way around, there is no access. You add those two up plus three or four other factors and again, all other things being equal, the common carrier will have a problem. So, either it goes out of business, which is unlikely, or the common carrier obligation is being whittled away at the margin under the guise of meeting competition and so on. That is an effect that's already been happening in the long-distance field for large users where bargaining and negotiations are taking place whatever the formal regulatory arrangement is. So the alternatives are to make private carriers common carriers, which is not realistic: it really means making every corporate, private network, every value-added service provider into a common carrier. You can also have some kind of a hybrid arrangement of which you can think in terms of at least 8 or 10 different hybrids. That is likely to work for a while, but eventually, the same dynamics take place. The private is going to push out the common carrier here, too, so a hybrid arrangement is not going to be a stable solution. If that is the case, then maybe common carriage as an institution in the long term is on its way out.

In speculating on the need to change common carriage arrangements, Noam posited that most of "the policy goals behind common carriage, which are free flow of information, limited liability, reduction of transaction costs, and a whole bunch of other things . . . will be taken care of in a competitive system of private carriers. . . . The ones that are not necessarily going to be taken care of involve the free flow of information aspect. That would then suggest not so much making everybody a common carrier, but rather making sure that no carrier can discriminate based on certain content criteria or some other long-term policy. This would be better than hanging on to the notion of common carriage per se."

Clearly, the debates over advancing the national information infrastructure underscore that development of nationwide networks will be very expensive; by one estimate, the physical facilities alone could consume $422 billion over 20 years.[20] In addition, the nation's reliance on the private sector for infrastructure investments demands that both public and private facilities be addressed in national policies (Egan and Wildman, 1992). Although volatile cost estimates reflect political considerations and business maneuvers, and although concerns have been raised about various risks, proponents argue that much of the investment would be made anyway,[21] and that the payback to investors (let alone to society generally) will be worth it.[22]

Apart from its controversial price-capping strategy—a relatively new approach to the regulation of information industries—the Cable Television Consumer Protection and Competition Act of 1992 demonstrates to members of the colloquium steering committee that Congress is often more amenable to retrospective "police" work than to forward-looking action on communications issues of the future. The chilling effect on cable-related investments and alliances ascribed to recent rate rollbacks is a cause for concern. And yet, even the Cable Act contained within it provisions that may have forward-looking impacts. For example, provisions relating to compatibility between cable service delivery and consumer electronics (TVs, VCRs) could serve to promote greater interoperability, notwithstanding industry concerns about specific mechanisms for doing so.

Noam elaborated on several points. The traditional telephone rate-subsidy system[23] will have to be restructured, he said, through some form of neutral surcharge and a voucher mechanism as a replacement for the present myriad pools, funds, and transfers. Through a principle of "third-party-neutral interconnection," a carrier could pick and choose its own customers, but it could not pick its customer's customers. This change will be brought on by increasing competition; providers will tend to compete for users who pay, and lower-revenue user groups will be left with fewer options and, as a result, with increasing prices. "These transitions will be painful. You'll hear from the losers, and [the transition] would require, therefore, leaders," Noam said. Competition will increase efficiency and hence reduce the magnitude of any subsidy, but it is not likely to decline to zero. Hence, we must reform the way it is being paid for, and reconcile it with competition. One idea, for example, is for every company providing telephone service to contribute in proportion to its customer base.[24]

Gilder, on the other hand, argued that the need for subsidies will disappear altogether, because digital wireless technology will reduce cost disparities between rural and urban services. This view is not universally accepted, given the bandwidth limitations of wireless technology. But Gilder's optimism about available bandwidth leads him to anticipate the obsolescence of the entire regulatory and legislative structure that controls information services (Kelly, 1993). In its auctions of spectrum for personal communications services (PCS), the FCC designed the auction so that even rural regions will have at least five major cellular and PCS providers. This approach should speed investment and lower prices.

The issue of how to assure universal service in a competitive marketplace also requires attention. As the information infrastructure evolves, people have begun to ask whether it will close or widen the gap between the rich and the poor. The Clinton administration has said it is "committed to developing a broad, modern concept of universal service—one that would emphasize giving all Americans who desire it easy, affordable access to advanced communications and information services, regardless of income, disability, or location" (IITF, 1993, p. 8). The progress during 1993-1994 of various new service trials, administration policy statements and explorations through the Information Infrastructure Task Force and the National Information Infrastructure Advisory Committee,[25] and legislative debates point to the difficulty of defining what it is that should be universally available. Mused Robert Johnson when interviewed,

> Clearly there should be a level at which everybody should have access to the service. Now, access is different from ability to use. Everybody can have access to cable television, but should it be pay-per-view cable television, should it be 50 channels, or 100 channels, or should it be all the other things that go along with it? Should everyone have the shopping channel? Should everyone get a remote for each room? You know, all of these things come into play when you start talking about an entitlement. I think the government should decide that there should be an entitlement for a certain level of access, but beyond that I think you get into trouble in deciding how much.

It is difficult, for example, to identify what kinds of information may relate to different kinds of gaps in socioeconomic status; it is difficult to build a case for mandating simultaneous access to a broad range of new services when experimentation and exploration of what kinds of services will be most popular and how costs can be optimized are still at early stages.[26]

Borrus, more optimistic than Noam about the future of common carriage, suggested that different types of carriers be assigned different responsibilities:

> Maybe what we're talking about is different levels of obligation, different levels of performance requirements, privacy requirements and other things including access to intellectual property based on the kind of network and service that you're providing—providers of physical networks being held to one standard, providers of virtual networks over physical networks to another standard. At the margins that runs into all the problems Eli talks about, but there are compensations for owning versus not owning, for managing and controlling a virtual [infrastructure] versus actually owning physical infrastructure. This debate has just begun.

OTHER USEFUL ROLES FOR GOVERNMENT

Regardless of how policymakers seek to guide or control information industries, the federal government can play a valuable role in promoting technological progress in other ways. In particular, colloquium participants stressed the effectiveness of procurement policies in improving government efficiency and diffusing new technologies throughout the economy.

Noting that the federal government is a major force in technology development,[27] Gilder suggested that government's role in the digital convergence should be that of an "aggressive, forward-looking consumer," purchasing the best possible technologies for interconnecting its supercomputer centers and other facilities. Such connections would maximize efficiency, according to Gilder, who has contended that the government typically "discovers a technology after its moment is passing" (Kelly, 1993). Gilder's comments echo other discussions about how the effectiveness of the federal investment in the Internet, whose backbone initially connected a variety of research and education facilities, contrasts with other federal efforts to promote specific technologies for government use, such as the Open Systems Interconnection protocol suite through the GOSIP federal information processing standard.

Borrus also has pointed to the influence of procurement policies. In assessing federal research and development (R&D) sponsorship in general, Borrus has contended that direct federal support historically has been less important to the success of commercial technology than have federal procurement and indirect support, because the latter approaches have tended to diffuse new technologies into widespread use.[28] On the other hand, the administration's National Performance Review (Clinton and Gore, 1993) and perennial efforts by adminstrations and the Congress to improve procurement policy and practice attest to the fact that procurement can be at best a blunt instrument. Also, the blossoming of the U.S. computer and communications enterprise provides evidence of the long-term fruits of federal R&D support overall (CSTB, 1995).

To further foster growth of the information infrastructure, Borrus suggested that policymakers consider how to stimulate experiments involving new technologies, configurations, and services, so that new applications and demand can emerge to support further evolution of the network portfolio. Similarly, Noam suggested that the government provide seed money for demonstration projects, as the National Science Foundation (NSF), the Advanced Research Projects Agency (ARPA), and other agencies have done. For example, NSF and ARPA contributed $15.8 million to the Gigabit Testbed program, which involved researchers from universities, national laboratories, supercomputer centers, and telephone and computer companies (CNRI, 1992). More generally, several colloquium participants identified the Internet as a working model for the type of experiment the federal government could support.[29] Experiments and demonstrations can help overcome a basic obstacle to network development: until a network is established, its usefulness is difficult to prove, but a sponsor must pay for the project first. "So you run into the catch-22 where you can't develop demand until you're willing to pay for the network, but no one is willing to pay for the network until you've got some demand developed," Borrus explained.

At the same time, Borrus noted, oversight is needed to "permit a kind of a logical infrastructure to emerge which would emphasize standards for access interoperability between these various pieces of the network portfolio—levels of privacy, reliability, performance standards, and the like—but which wouldn't determine the actual implementation of any of the networks themselves." The National Cable Television Association (NCTA) has provided specific suggestions along those lines, arguing that local telephone companies should be required to "interconnect their facilities with those of more specialized providers on reasonable and nondiscriminatory terms" (NCTA, 1993a). NCTA also supports a federal role in standards setting for networks and customer equipment, to ensure, for example, that computers and telephones can send and receive cable signals and programming, as well as tax incentives to stimulate investment (NCTA, 1993a). The current fiscal climate makes it relative unlikely that tax incentives will be initiated. Moreover, whether and what kind of oversight is possible to achieve logical connectivity and so on is a challenge at the heart of public policy for advancing the information infrastructure: it is a challenge that many recognize but few can resolve to the satisfaction of the majority.

Commercial activities in the Internet arena have built on contributions to the technology base through federal research programs (such as the High Performance Computing and Communications Initiative) as well as development by private enterprise. However, competition, deregulation, and industry consolidation appear to have reduced telecommunications industry R&D from what it was in the heyday of AT&T's Bell Laboratories and in the early years of Bellcore. Thus Wildman has noted that U.S. telephone companies lag their foreign counterparts in R&D spending and patent activity (Egan and Wildman, 1992).[30] The combined forces of deficit-reduction pressures and a policy shift toward applications may constrain federally funded research in related technologies. Any slowdown in research would be particularly troubling now, because integrating diverse systems to evolve the nation's information infrastructure poses new technical challenges, some associated with lowering the costs of providing more general and flexible technology as compared to more specialized technology that is optimized for the delivery of a single service (CSTB, 1994b).

As noted in earlier chapters, a valuable part of the infrastructure is the content—the software and the programming. Thus, it is important for the government to support experiments focusing not only on networking hardware, but also on applications. Part of the appeal of the Internet, it should be noted, is that users develop their own "programming" and other information resources, from articles to databases, resources that can be located and interconnected increasingly easily through the search and navigation tools (e.g., gopher, World Wide Web) that are themselves being developed by users (Berners-Lee et al., 1994).

NOTES

1. The administration envisions national high-speed networks capable of transmitting billions of bits (gigabits) of information—such as the entire textual portion of the *Encyclopedia Britannica*—in one second. These networks would link computers, data banks, fax machines, telephones, and video displays.

In its national information infrastructure (NII) policy statements, the administration has articulated a high-level vision for a "network of networks" funded primarily by the private sector. The statements outline numerous broad goals but provide few details; the Information Infrastructure Task Force is laying the groundwork to develop proposals in a number of areas, and proposed legislation is proceeding through the Congress as this report is written. The organization of several budget elements under the NII umbrella in the FY 1995 budget request added to the emphasis on this area, as do the new emphasis on information infrastructure technology and applications within the High Performance Computing and Communications Initiative and the expansion of the new Telecommunications and Information Infrastructure Assistance Program for developing access by schools, libraries, hospitals, and clinics.

2. Common carriers provide neutral, nondiscriminatory service. They are subject to public utility regulations described by Kahn (1970, p. 3) as "control of entry, price fixing, prescription of quality and conditions of service, and the imposition of an obligation to serve all applicants under reasonable conditions."

3. Lobbying activity is so intense that it itself has become a news item. See, for example, Andrews (1995).

4. Section 310(b) of the Communications Act limits foreign investment in U.S. broadcasting companies to 25 percent.

5. For example, several measures show that Japan lags the United States in use of communications and information technology, even accounting for population difference: PCs used in business per 100 workers (U.S. 41.7, Japan 9.9); domestic commercial databases (U.S. 3,900, Japan 900); Internet nodes (U.S. 1.18 million, Japan 39,000); LAN connections per 100 PCs used in business (U.S. 55.7, Japan 13.4); cellular phones per 100 people (U.S. 4.4, Japan 1.4); and cable (non-basic service) subscribers as percent of households with TV (U.S. 60 percent, Japan 2.7 percent).

Regulation-supported high prices and market structure factors lie behind some of these conditions (Pollack, 1993).

6. Principles quoted from "The G7 Theme Paper," a document found on the World Wide Web at http://www.ispo.cec.be (EC Information Society Project Office Webserver) under *G7 Information Society Conference* category and *Key Documents* subcategory.

7. Foreign investors have taken advantage of the opportunity to invest in U.S. companies, notably in the entertainment industry. For example, News Corp. of Australia owns (20th Century) Fox Inc., Sony Corp. owns Sony Pictures Entertainment (formerly Columbia Pictures), and Matsushita Electric Industrial Co. owns MCA Inc. (parent company of Universal Pictures). See Turner (1994a).

8. An extensive analysis of the *keiretsu* system may be found in Gerlach (1992).

9. Virtually every major nation has signed the convention, which is administered by the World Intellectual Property Organization.

10. Further analysis of these national differences may be found in Cowhey (1993).

11. See CSTB (1992) for a discussion of the business of systems integration.

12. Colloquium steering committee member Janice Obuchowski noted that, at the time of the consent decree, AT&T indicated no objection to the Bell companies entering the information content business, and the court concluded they would not abuse any residual bottleneck power in information services. In addition, the court observed that the FCC had established safeguards that would help protect against such abuse.

13. If these types of incentives prove inadequate, then policymakers could consider other measures, such as a value-added tax (VAT) on public network services, with the proceeds to be invested in the public infrastructure, Wildman suggested. An advantage of the VAT approach, he noted, is that the major beneficiaries—end users and suppliers—would pay (Egan and Wildman, 1992).

14. The regional Bell holding companies have promised, if the restrictions on cable programming and long-distance service are relaxed, to invest an additional $100 billion in advanced technology in the next decade—precisely the sort of private investment needed to advance a national information infrastructure.

15. In 1992, the FCC modified its 1970 rule that prevented networks from owning cable systems (47 CFR 76.501[a][1991]) to allow cross-ownership so long as the number of cable homes affected was limited. Networks have been barred by the Cable Act of 1984 (47 USC Section 533) from owning cable systems in their own markets where they own and operate stations (NTIA, 1993). Progress through judicial and regulatory hurdles toward video dial-tone service is reflected in Bell Atlantic's moves toward offering cable-like programming in its service areas (Landler, 1995; Carnevale, 1994).

16. In 1970, the FCC adopted a rule barring common ownership of a television broadcast station and a cable system in the same market (47 CFR Section 76.501[a][2]). Congress codified that rule in the Cable Act of 1984 (NTIA, 1993).

17. The FCC adopted a 12-station limit for all broadcast services in 1984.

18. David Nicoll, National Cable Television Association, personal communication, December 13, 1993.

19. Ameritech, for example, proposed a new regulatory model (the Customers First Plan) under which the corporation would guarantee its competitors physical access to the telephone network and fair pricing; all that a competitor would have to do is buy a switch (costing several million dollars new). Ameritech also pledged to upgrade its network to support digital switching and fiber optics. In return, Ameritech asked for "the freedom to fully compete, including the ability to de-average all access rates, to respond to competitive proposals, and to enter into contracts with customers" (Ameritech, 1993c). Local telephone service would remain affordable, the company said, due to increased usage of telecommunications services.

20. Carol Weinhaus, project director for the Center for Telecommunications Management at the University of Southern California, cited in Andrews (1994a).

21. Local telephone and cable companies already spend about $25 billion a year on new equipment and modernization (Federal Communications Commission estimates, cited in Andrews (1994a)). A number of telephone companies announced ambitious infrastructure improvement plans in 1993.

22. The Clinton administration, in its national information infrastructure (NII) policy statement, noted that an estimated two-thirds of U.S. workers hold information-related

jobs, while the rest work in industries that rely heavily on information. According to the administration, the NII "will help create high-wage jobs, stimulate economic growth, enable new products and services, and strengthen America's technological leadership. Whole new industries will be created, and the infrastructure will be used in ways we can only begin to imagine" (IITF, 1993, p. 13). A number of statistics were cited to bolster this contention. For example, the Computer Systems Policy Project estimates that the NII will produce as much as $300 billion annually in new sales across multiple industries. And the personal communications services industry, a new family of wireless services, is expected to create as many as 300,000 jobs in the next 10 to 15 years.

23. According to the United States Telephone Association (USTA), regulatory policy promoting universal service has resulted in up to $20 billion in internal subsidies that benefit rural and residential customers. USTA (1993) has claimed that, as competition in the marketplace increases, the price of local telephone service would move to cost and could double.

24. David Nicoll, National Cable Television Association, personal communication, December 13, 1993.

25. Several public meetings (e.g., the 20/20 Vision and Public Interest conferences) were held and documents issued for public discussion and comment in 1994.

26. For example, NTIA estimates that the biggest problems in regard to universal service pertain to the urban poor, even though infrastructure is cheap and ubiquitous, not rural areas.

27. The federal government finances some $70 billion in research and development annually and creates early markets for high-risk technologies such as computer hardware and semiconductors (Clinton and Gore, 1993).

28. In this paper (Borrus, 1992), echoing a decade-old recommendation made by the economist Richard Nelson and his colleagues (Nelson, 1982), Borrus suggested that the government associate research and development (R&D) support with procurement or other well-defined public objectives; define and fund arenas of nonproprietary research and allow the scientific community to guide R&D allocation; and develop mechanisms whereby potential users guide the allocation of applied R&D funds. Borrus made several additional points, specifying conditions that should exist for applied research and the importance of pursuing widespread diffusion of new technologies within the domestic economy. He also stressed the importance of ensuring that the development process produces technology that meets commercial market requirements.

29. Over the years, the government's role in running the Internet has been reduced. The initial goal was to link military users and contractors with remote computer centers so they could share software and hardware; today, more than half the hosts are commercial, while many others are in education and nonmilitary research. The National Science Foundation has provided the fixed-cost network "backbone," but by early 1994 the direct federal subsidy had shrunk to an estimated 3 percent of total Internet costs, and even that small share is to be eliminated. Meanwhile, standards for transmission, user interfaces, management, and other aspects of Internet use are set through a "grass-roots" process led by the Internet Engineering Task Force, whose meetings are open to anyone with a demonstrated working protocol. Howard Funk, the Internet Society, personal communication, November 10, 1993.

30. Egan and Wildman (1992) citing NTIA (1991). The seven nations evaluated included the United States, the United Kingdom, Germany, France, Italy, Japan, and Canada.

Bibliography

Ameritech. 1992. *SuperSchools: Education in the Information Age and Beyond.* Ameritech, Chicago, Ill.

Ameritech. 1993a. *Evaluation of ThinkLink: January through June, 1993.* July 28. Evaluators June Cline, Richard Omanson, and Project Manager Nancy Sisung. Ameritech, Chicago, Ill.

Ameritech. 1993b. "Nation's Public Phone Network Can Be the Right Medicine to Trim U.S. Health Care Costs and Improve Delivery." News release dated August 5.

Ameritech. 1993c. "Petition for Declaratory Ruling and Related Waivers to Establish a New Regulatory Model for the Ameritech Region," petition before the Federal Communications Commission, March 1.

Ameritech. 1993d. *Project ThinkLink: Educational Applications for FITL.* Ameritech, Chicago, Ill., November.

Ameritech. 1993e. *Quality of Life in the Information Age and Beyond.* Ameritech, Chicago, Ill., March.

Ameritech. 1993f. "SuperSchool—America's Link to a Better Education—Comes to Washington, D.C., March 24-31." News release dated March 11.

Andrews, Edmund L. 1993. "When We Build It, Will They Come?," *New York Times,* October 17, p. F5.

Andrews, Edmund L. 1994a. "Big Risk and Cost Seen in Creating Data Superhighway," *New York Times,* January 3, p. C17.

Andrews, Edmund L. 1994b. "With Merger's Failure, an Industry Seeks a Leader," *New York Times,* February 26, p. A39.

Andrews, Edmund L. 1995. "Phone-Bill Lobbyists Wear out Welcome," *New York Times,* March 20, pp. D1 and D6.

Associated Press. 1994. "Packard Bell to Offer PC Cum TV/Phone/Radio," *New York Times,* June 14, p. D5.

Bangemann, Martin (Chair), and the High-Level Group on the Information Society. 1994. *Europe and the Global Information Society: Recommendations to the European Council.* European Council, Brussels, May 26.

Barron, James. 1994. "A New Species of Couch Potato Takes Root," *New York Times,* November 6, pp. H1 and H28.

Bermant, Charles. 1994. "When Listener and Artist Can Make Music Together," *New York Times,* May 8, p. F9.

Bermant, Charles. 1995. "Letting Moviegoers Play Auteur, with a Clicker," *New York Times,* February 12, p. F10.

Berners-Lee, Tim, Robert Cailliau, Ari Luotonen, Henrik Frystyk Nielsen, and Arthur Secret. 1994. "The World-Wide Web," *Communications of the ACM* 37(8):76-82.

Booker, Ellis. 1994. "Throwing Users an Mbone," *Computerworld,* November 7, pp. 63 and 68.

Borrus, Michael. 1992. "Investing on the Frontier: How the U.S. Can Reclaim High-Tech Leadership," *American Prospect,* Fall issue, pp. 79-87.

Borrus, Michael 1993. "The Regional Architecture of Global Electronics: Trajectories, Linkages and Access to Technology," pp. 41-80 in *New Challenges to International Cooperation: Adjustment of Firms, Policies, and Organizations to Global Competition,* Peter Gourevitch and Paolo Guerrieri, eds. International Relations and Pacific Studies, University of California, San Diego.

Bowles, Scott. 1994. "Cyberspace Rescue Prevents a Suicide," *Washington Post,* October 24, pp. D1 and D5.

Bulkeley, William M. 1995. "Untested Treatments, Cures Find Stronghold on On-Line Services," *Wall Street Journal,* February 27, pp. A1 and A9.

Bulkeley, William M., and John R. Wilke. 1993. "Can the Exalted Vision Become Reality?: Early Attempts Show Buyers May Be Leery," *Wall Street Journal,* October 14, pp. B1 and B12.

Burgess, John. 1994. "Computers Get a Blockbuster Role," *Washington Post,* January 19, pp. F1 and F4.

Carlton, Jim. 1994a. "As Electronics Lag, Computers Step into Breach," *Wall Street Journal,* January 5, p. B1.

Carlton, Jim. 1994b. "CD-ROMs: Buggy, Boring, Slow, Frustrating," *Wall Street Journal,* July 6, pp. B1 and B4.

Carlton, Jim. 1994c. "Electronic Arts Shifts Focus to CD-ROM Video Games," *Wall Street Journal,* September 7, p. B4.

Carlton, Jim. 1994d. "3DO Faces Revolt by Game Developers over Fee to Cut Manufacturers' Losses," *Wall Street Journal,* October 24, p. B3.

Carlton, Jim, and Thomas R. King. 1994. "Sega-MGM Pact Will Prompt Question: Which Came First, Movie or Video Game?," *Wall Street Journal,* April 27, p. B8.

Carnevale, Mary Lu. 1994. "Bell Atlantic Becomes First Phone Firm Allowed to Compete with Cable TV," *Wall Street Journal,* July 7, pp. A3 and A5.

Cauley, Leslie. 1993. "Goal: No Missing Link," *USA TODAY,* June 9, p. 2B.

Chartrand, Sabra. 1994. "Patents: The Promise of a Multimedia Revolution Is Creating a Giant Copyright Headache for Some Companies," *New York Times,* March 28, p. D2.

Chiddix, James A. 1991. "The Evolution of Cable TV—A Personal Perspective," lecture at Pennsylvania State University, October 29.

Churbuck, David C. 1994. "Dial-a-catalog," *Forbes* 154(8):126-130.

Clinton, William J., and Albert Gore, Jr. 1993. *Technology for America's Strength: A New Direction to Build Economic Strength.* U.S. Government Printing Office, Washington, D.C.

Computer Science and Telecommunications Board (CSTB), National Research Council. 1992. *Keeping the U.S. Computer Industry Competitive: Systems Integration.* National Academy Press, Washington, D.C.

Computer Science and Telecommunications Board (CSTB), National Research Council. 1994a. *Information Technology in the Service Society: A Twenty-first Century Lever.* National Academy Press, Washington, D.C.

Computer Science and Telecommunications Board (CSTB), National Research Council. 1994b. *Realizing the Information Future: The Internet and Beyond.* National Academy Press, Washington, D.C.

Computer Science and Telecommunications Board (CSTB), National Research Council. 1994c. *Rights and Responsibilities of Participants in Networked Communities.* National Academy Press, Washington, D.C.

Computer Science and Telecommunications Board (CSTB), National Research Council. 1995. *Evolving the High Performance Computing and Communications Initiative to Support the Nation's Information Infrastructure.* National Academy Press, Washington, D.C.

Corcoran, Cate. 1993. "Spectrum Envoy Card Gives PC-Phone Link for Faxes, Voice Mail," *Infoworld,* November 8, p. 34.

Corcoran, Elizabeth. 1994. "A 'Battle of the Box' Is Brewing," *Washington Post,* October 15, pp. D1-D2.

Corporation for National Research Initiatives (CNRI). 1992. "A Brief Description of the CNRI Gigabit Testbed Initiative." Corporation for National Research Initiatives, Reston, Va., January.

Council on Competitiveness (COC). 1993. *Roadmap for Results: Trade Policy, Technology, and American Competitiveness.* Council on Competitiveness, Washington, D.C., July.

Cowhey, Peter F. 1990. "The International Telecommunications Regime: The Political Roots of Regimes for High Technology," *International Organization* 44(2):169-199.

Cowhey, Peter F. 1993. "Telecommunications: Market Access Regimes in Services and Equipment," pp. 133-170 in *New Challenges to International Cooperation: Adjustment of Firms, Policies, and Organizations to Global Competition,* Peter Gourevitch and Paolo Guerrieri, eds. International Relations and Pacific Studies, University of California, San Diego.

Cowhey, Peter F., and Jonathan D. Aronson. 1993. *Managing the World Economy: The Consequences of Corporate Alliances.* Council on Foreign Relations Press, New York.

David, Fred. 1993. "I Want My Desktop MTV," *Wired* 3(1):84.

Dreier, Thomas. 1993. "Copyright Digitized: Philosophical Impacts and Practical Implications for Information Exchange in Digital Networks," paper presented at "World Intellectual Property Organization Symposium on the Impact of Digital Technology on Copyright and Neighboring Rights," Harvard University, March 31-April 2.

Dukes, S.D. n.d. *Next Generation Cable Network Architecture.* Cable Television Laboratories Inc., Boulder, Colo. (unpublished).

Dutton, William H., Jay G. Blumler, and Kenneth L. Kraemer. 1987. *Wired Cities: Shaping the Future of Communications.* G.K. Hall, Boston.

The Economist. 1993a. "A Survey of Telecommunications," 329(7834):a special supplement following p. 68.

The Economist. 1993b. "What 3DO Might Do: Home Entertainment, Tripping," 327(7815):80.

Egan, Bruce L., and Steven S. Wildman. 1992. "Investing in the Telecommunications Infrastructure: Economics and Policy Considerations," pp. 19-54 in *A National Information Network: Changing Our Lives in the 21st Century.* Annual Review of the Institute for Information Studies (Northern Telecom Inc. and the Aspen Institute), Queenstown, Md.

Elmer-DeWitt, Philip. 1993. "Take a Trip into the Future on the Electronic Superhighway," *Time* 141(15):50-55.

Eriksson, Hans. 1994. "MBone: The Multicast Backbone," *Communications of the ACM* 37(8):54-60.

Fabrikant, Geraldine. 1993. "Bell Atlantic's Acquisition Presented as a Quantum Leap," *New York Times,* October 14, p. D11.

Fantel, Hans. 1994. "Cinema Sound Gets a Digital Lift," *New York Times,* June 12, p. F9.

Farhi, Paul. 1994. "A Waiting Game for Rating Games," *Washington Post,* December 24, p. D1.

Farhi, Paul, and Sandra Sugawara. 1994. "Hurdles Slow Information 'Superhypeway,'" *Washington Post*, April 7, pp. A1 and A15.

Farley, Christopher John. 1994. "Patriot Games," *TIME Magazine*, December 19, p. 48.

Fisher, Lawrence M. 1994. "Disney Licenses Characters for Multimedia," *New York Times*, June 24, p. D6.

Fitzgerald, Michael. 1994. "Multimedia Is Growing by Leaps and Bounds," *Computerworld*, February 21, p. 42.

Flaherty, Joseph A. 1993. "HDTV: How, Why, and When," The Schoenberg Lecture presented for the Royal Television Society at the Royal Institution, London, England, November 4.

Flaherty, Joseph A. 1994. "ATV: How to Do It, Whatever It Is," paper presented at the Advanced Television seminar "Bit by Bit into the Future," Hilton Head, South Carolina, September 27.

Fleischmann, Mark. 1995. "Second Sight," *Premiere* 8(5):90.

Flynn, Laurie. 1994. "CD-ROM's: They're Not Just for Entertainment," *New York Times*, April 24, p. F10.

Foderaro, Lisa W. 1995. "Self-Help Today: I'm OK. You're OK. We're On Line," *New York Times*, March 22, pp. B1 and B6.

Garreau, Joel. 1993. "Bawdy Bytes: The Growing World of Cybersex," *Washington Post*, November 29, p. A1.

Gerlach, Michael L. 1992. *Alliance Capitalism: The Social Organization of Japanese Business*. University of California Press, Berkeley, Calif.

Goldberg, Michael. 1993. "Attack of the Cyber-Rockers: New Computer Rocker Jocks Get Their Modems Working," *Rolling Stone*, November 25, No. 670, p. 27.

Harmon, Amy. 1993. "The 'Seedy' Side of CD-ROMs," *Los Angeles Times*, November 29, pp. A1 and A26-A28.

Herschman, N. 1993. "CD Sound Gets Better," *Pulse*, August, No. 117, p. 20.

Hill, G. Christian, and Ken Yamada. 1993. "Five Electronics Giants Hope General Magic Will Turn the Trick," *Wall Street Journal*, February 8, p. A1.

Hodge, Winston William. 1995. *Interactive Television: A Comprehensive Guide for Multimedia Technologists*. McGraw-Hill Inc., New York.

Hudson, Richard L. 1994. "Europe Begins Liberalizing Phone Sector," *Wall Street Journal*, December 5, p. A9A.

Hudson, Richard L. 1995. "License Needed to Do Art Deals in Digital Age," *Wall Street Journal*, January 23, pp. B1-B2.

Hudson, Richard L., and James Pressley. 1995. "G-7 Nations Make Gains in Facilitating Access to Information Superhighway," *Wall Street Journal*, February 27, p. A7A.

Huizinga, Johan. 1950. *Homo Ludens: A Study of the Play Element in Culture*. Beacon Press, Boston.

Information & Interactive Services Report (IISR). 1995. "Worldwide Internet Creates Potential for Legal Problems," BRP Publications Inc., Washington, D.C., March 24, p. 18.

Information Infrastructure Task Force (IITF). 1993. *The National Information Infrastructure: Agenda for Action*. Information Infrastructure Task Force, Washington, D.C., September 15.

Institute for Information Studies. 1995. *Crossroads on the Information Highway: Convergence and Diversity in Communications Technologies*. Annual Review of the Institute for Information Studies (Northern Telecom Inc. and the Aspen Institute), Queenstown, Md.

Jensen, Elizabeth. 1994. "Networks Pick UCLA to Study Violence, Hoping to Pre-empt Government Action," *Wall Street Journal*, June 30, p. B9.

Johnson, Bradley. 1993. "Multimedia PC Biz Picking up Speed," *Advertising Age* 64(23):6.

Kahn, Alfred E. 1970. *The Economics of Regulation: Principles and Institutions, Volume 1*. John Wiley & Sons Inc., New York.

Kapor, Mitchell. 1993. "Where Is the Digital Highway Really Heading?," *Wired* 1(3):53.

Karlgaard, Rich. 1994. "More (Moore) Fights to Come," *Forbes*, February 28 (Supplemental), p. 9.

Katz, Michael L., and Carl Shapiro. 1994. "Systems Competition and Network Effects," *Journal of Economic Perspectives* 8(2):93-115.

Keller, John J. 1994. "AT&T Scraps Plan to Sell Gear for Video Game," *Wall Street Journal,* September 1, p. B8.

Kelly, Kevin. 1993. "When Bandwidth Is Free: The Dark Fiber Interview with George Gilder," *Wired* 1(4):38-41.

Kelly, Kevin, and Rheingold, Howard. 1993. "The Dragon Ate My Homework," *Wired* 1(3):69.

Kim, James, and Chris Wloszczyna. 1993. "Hitting the Information Highway," *USA TODAY,* August 26, p. 4B.

King, Jr., Ralph T. 1994. "3DO Faces Struggle to Keep Video-Game Player Alive," *Wall Street Journal,* May 19, p. B4.

Klein, Stanley, and Robert Aston. 1993. "Multimedia Defined: Market Sectors, Dimensions, and Directions," pp. 7-35 in *Multimedia 2000: Market Developments, Media Business Impacts, and Future Trends,* M.L. De Sonne, ed. National Association of Broadcasters, Washington, D.C.

Kolbert, Elizabeth. 1994. "Television Gets Closer Look As a Factor in Real Violence," *New York Times,* December 14, pp. A1 and D20.

Kristol, Irving. 1994. "Sex, Violence and Videotape," *Wall Street Journal,* May 31, p. A16.

Kruger, Pamela. 1994. "The Multimedia Job Mirage," *New York Times,* January 9, p. F9.

Laderman, Jeffrey M., Mark Landler, and Ronald Grover. 1993. "Media Mania," *Business Week,* July 12, No. 3327, pp. 110-119.

Landis, David. 1993. "New Wave of Interactive Entertainment," *USA Today,* May 27, p. 1D.

Landler, Mark. 1995. "Phone Companies Clear TV Hurdle," *New York Times,* March 18, pp. 1 and 41.

Lanham, Richard A. 1993. *The Electronic Word: Democracy, Technology, and the Arts.* University of Chicago Press, Chicago, Ill.

Lashinsky, Adam. 1993. "Amanda and Ameritech: 10-year-olds Serve as the Ultimate Focus Group," *Crain's Detroit Business,* September 6, p. 13.

Lavin, Douglas. 1995. "Survey Sees Cost of Telephone Calls for Business Dropping in Most Nations," *Wall Street Journal,* March 3, p. A5C.

Lewis, Peter H. 1993a. "Multimedia (Especially the X-Rated) Stars at Comdex," *New York Times,* November 23, p. F12.

Lewis, Peter H. 1993b. "The New Patent That Is Infuriating the Multimedia Industry: The Battle over a Popular Way of Searching Data Bases," *New York Times,* November 28, p. F10.

Lewis, Peter H. 1994a. "A Boom for On-Line Services," *New York Times,* July 12, pp. D1 and D14.

Lewis, Peter H. 1994b. "Prodigy Cuts Work Force As Part of Broad Revamping," *New York Times,* December 6, p. D5.

Lippman, John. 1993. "Gambling—Literally—on the Media Superhighway," *Los Angeles Times,* December 24, pp. D1 and D4.

Lippman, John, and Amy Harmon. 1994. "Gore Presides at L.A. Summit on Info Age," *Los Angeles Times,* January 12, pp. A1 and A19.

Lohr, Steve. 1994. "The Silver Disk May Soon Eclipse the Silver Screen," *New York Times,* March 1, pp. A1 and D6.

Lubove, Seth, and Neil Weinberg. 1993. "Creating a Seamless Company," *Forbes* 152(14):152-157.

Maney, Kevin. 1993. "Ruling Opens Door to Union of Telephone, Cable, Video: Consumers Likely to See More Choices," *USA TODAY,* August 25, p. 1B.

Markoff, John. 1993. "Cable Concerns in Venture to Rival Phone Companies," *New York Times,* December 2, p. D1.

Markoff, John. 1994. "For 3DO, a Make-or-Break Season," *New York Times,* December 11, pp. F1 and F6.

Markoff, John. 1995a. "Another Format War Looms in Video Recording Industry," *New York Times,* February 23, pp. D1 and D17.

Markoff, John. 1995b. "Will Video Game Machines Turn into PC Killers?," *New York Times,* January 8, p. F7.

Marsh, Barbara. 1994. "Musicians Adopt Technology to Market Their Skills," *Wall Street Journal,* October 14, p. B2.

McCartney, Scott. 1995. "Hollywood, Silicon Valley Team up—and Clash," *Wall Street Journal,* March 14, pp. B1-B2.

McCoy, Charles. 1994. "Hewlett, CBS to Unveil Pact for Digital TV," *Wall Street Journal,* August 30, p. B10.

McMurray, Scott. 1994. "Television Shopping Is Stepping up in Class," *New York Times,* March 6, p. F5.

Memmott, Mark, and Kevin Maney. 1993. "USA Poised to Be Multimedia Superpower," *USA TODAY,* October 15, p. B1.

Millison, Doug, and Craig LaGrow. 1993. "Multimedia 'Black Boxes:' Advent of the Digital Media Home," pp. 103-120 in *Multimedia 2000: Market Developments, Media Business Impacts, and Future Trends,* M.L. De Sonne, ed. National Association of Broadcasters, Washington, D.C.

Mohan, Suruchi. 1994. "Multimedia to Run on Chip," *Computerworld,* October 3, p. 12.

Mohan, Suruchi, and Jean S. Bozman. 1994. "Race for Multimedia Crown Speeding up: Companies Team to Get Jump on Interactive Services," *Computerworld,* June 27, p. 12.

National Cable Television Association (NCTA). 1993a. *Cable Television and America's Telecommunications Infrastructure.* National Cable Television Association, Washington, D.C.

National Cable Television Association (NCTA). 1993b. *Interactive Surgery Demonstration; Linking: An Idea Exchange for Cable Professionals.* National Cable Television Association, Washington, D.C., July.

National Cable Television Association (NCTA). 1993c. *Twenty First Century Television: Cable Television in the Information Age.* National Cable Television Association, Washington, D.C.

National Telecommunications and Information Administration (NTIA). 1991. *The NTIA Infrastructure Report: Telecommunications in the Age of Information.* U.S. Department of Commerce, Washington, D.C., October.

National Telecommunications and Information Administration (NTIA), U.S. Department of Commerce. 1993. *Globalization of the Mass Media.* U.S. Government Printing Office, Washington, D.C.

Nelson, Richard R. 1982. *Government and Technical Progress: A Cross-industry Analysis.* Pergamon Press, New York.

Newman, Melinda. 1994. "CDs Push Music Sales Past $10 Bil Mark," *Billboard,* March 5, p. 6.

New York Times. 1994. "Sony and Phillips Design CDs for Movies," December 17, p. 41.

Noam, Eli. 1995. "Beyond Telecommunications Liberalization: Past Performance, Present Hype, and Future Direction," *The New Information Infrastructure: Strategies for U.S. Policy,* William J. Drake, ed. Twentieth Century Fund Press, New York, forthcoming.

Oettinger, Anthony G. 1993. "Information Age Choices: The Ecstasy and the Agony," paper presented at the 1993 Asia-Pacific Conference on Communications, "Integrated Communications for Information Society," Taejon, Korea, August 25.

O'Neill, Molly. 1995. "The Lure and Addiction of Life on Line," *New York Times,* March 8, pp. C1 and C6.

Parkes, Walter. 1994. "Random Access, Remote Control: The Evolution of Storytelling," *Omni* 16(4):48-54.

Pereira, Joseph. 1994. "PC Games Could Capture Sega, Nintendo Customers," *Wall Street Journal,* April 27, pp. B1 and B8.

Perelman, Lewis J. 1993. "How Hypermation Leaps the Learning Curve," *Forbes,* October 25 (Supplemental), pp. 76-90.

Pitta, Julie. 1993. "Hyperinteractive," *Forbes* 152(6):228-230.

Pollack, Andrew. 1993. "Now It's Japan's Turn to Play Catch-up," *New York Times*, November 21, p. F1.

Radcliffe, Mark F. 1993. "Intellectual Property and Multimedia: Legal Issues in the New Media World," pp. 121-148 in *Multimedia 2000: Market Developments, Media Business Impacts, and Future Trends*, M.L. De Sonne, ed. National Association of Broadcasters, Washington, D.C.

Radiological Society of North America (RSNA). 1994. "National Library of Medicine Unveils 'The Visible Man': Computerized Cadaver Released onto the Internet." Press release dated November 28.

Ramirez, Anthony. 1993. "2 Groups Plan Projects on Computer Standards," *New York Times*, December 14, p. D5.

Reilly, Patrick M. 1994. "Home Shoppers to Be Given Yet Another Service," *Wall Street Journal*, January 14, p. B1.

Rheingold, Howard. 1993. *The Virtual Community: Homesteading on the Electronic Frontier.* Addison-Wesley Publishing Company, New York.

Rickard, Jack. 1993. "Home-grown BBS," *Wired* 1(4):42-45.

Rifkin, Glenn. 1993. "At Age 9, On-Line Service Reboots," *New York Times*, November 8, p. D1.

Robichaux, Mark, and Don Clark. 1994. "Time Warner Delays Launch of TV Service: Trial Interactive Network in Orlando Is Set Back by Problems at 2 Firms," *Wall Street Journal*, March 2, pp. A3-4.

Rosen, David. 1993. "Multimedia and Future Media: 2000 and Beyond," pp. 207-228 in *Multimedia 2000: Market Developments, Media Business Impacts, and Future Trends*, M.L. De Sonne, ed. National Association of Broadcasters, Washington, D.C.

Rothstein, Edward. 1994. "A New Art Form May Arise from the 'Myst,'" *New York Times*, December 4, pp. H1 and H24-25.

Samuels, Gary. 1994a. "CD-ROM's First Big Victim," *Forbes* 153(5):42-44.

Samuels, Gary. 1994b. "Partner or Die," *Forbes* 154(6):128-130.

Samuels, Gary. 1994c. "What Profits?," *Forbes* 154(10):74-78.

Schwartz, John. 1993. "Caution: Children at Play on Information Highway," *Washington Post*, November 28, p. A1.

Schwartz, John. 1994. "A Terminal Obsession: Nathaniel Davenport Lost Himself in Computer Games. And Then He Lost His Life. A Modern Cyberdrama," *Washington Post*, March 27, pp. F1 and F4.

Schwarz, Joyce. 1993. "Reinventing Hollywood: Creative Approaches to New Media Production," pp. 37-64 in *Multimedia 2000: Market Developments, Media Business Impacts, and Future Trends*, M.L. De Sonne, ed. National Association of Broadcasters, Washington, D.C.

Seigel, Jessica. 1994. "Computer Games? That's Hollywood!," *Washington Business*, July 25, pp. 15 and 19.

Shapiro, Eben. 1994. "Time Warner's Orlando Test to Start—Finally," *Wall Street Journal*, December 7, pp. B1 and B4.

Shrage, Michael. 1994. "East Is East, and West Is West, But Neither May Rule over New Media," *Washington Post*, June 26, p. F3.

Sims, Calvin. 1993. "PacTel Is Granted Approval to Spin off Its Wireless Unit," *New York Times*, November 3, p. D1.

Sims, Calvin. 1994. "For Consumers, Multimedia Shines," *New York Times*, January 10, p. D1.

Solomon, Jolie. 1993. "A Risky Revolution," *Newsweek* 121(17):44-45.

Sugawara, Sandra, and Paul Farhi. 1993. "Merger to Create a Media Giant," *Washington Post*, October 14, p. A1.

Tetzeli, Rick. 1993. "Videogames: Serious Fun," *Fortune* 128(16):110-116.

Turner, Richard. 1993a. "Hollywood Is Seeing the Future, and It Is Interactive Show Biz," *Wall Street Journal*, May 19, p. A1.

Turner, Richard. 1993b. "Video-Game Innovator Lures Corporate Giants to 'Interactive' Media," *Wall Street Journal,* February 7, p. A1.

Turner, Richard. 1994a. "Hollywired," *Wall Street Journal,* March 21, pp. R1 and R6.

Turner, Richard. 1994b. "Walt Disney Will Announce Its Plans to Produce and Market Video Games," *Wall Street Journal,* December 5, p. B4B.

Turner, Richard, and Thomas R. King. 1993. "Disney Stands Aside as Rivals Stampede to Digital Alliances," *Wall Street Journal,* September 24, p. A1.

United States Telephone Association (USTA). 1993. "USTA Calls for Responsible Transition to Competition in Local Telephone Markets." Press release dated July 28.

U.S. Department of Commerce (DOC). 1993. *U.S. Industrial Outlook 1993.* U.S. Government Printing Office, Washington, D.C.

Washington Post. 1993. "Pacific Bell Revamping Network: Big Multimedia System Planned," November 12, pp. G1 and G3.

Washington Post. 1995. "America Online Reports a Loss," February 9, p. D11.

Weber, Thomas E. 1994. "GE's GEnie Hopes Ads Can Work Magic to Boost Membership of On-Line Service," *Wall Street Journal,* February 14, p. B4.

Wildman, Steven S., and Stephen E. Siwek. 1988. *International Trade in Films and Television Programs.* Ballinger, Cambridge, Mass.

Women's-Wear-Daily (WWD). 1994. "Bear Bullish on TV Shopping," May 10, p. 19.

Woo, Junda. 1993. "Publisher Sues CompuServe over a Song," *Wall Street Journal,* December 16, pp. B1 and B16.

Yadon, Robert E. 1993. "Broadcasting and Multimedia: Operations, Applications, Opportunities," pp. 149-171 in *Multimedia 2000: Market Developments, Media Business Impacts, and Future Trends,* M.L. De Sonne, ed. National Association of Broadcasters, Washington, D.C.

Zachary, G. Pascal. 1994. "Microsoft Sets Stock Purchase of Softimage," *Wall Street Journal,* February 15, p. B5.

Ziegler, Bart. 1994a. "Five Technology Concerns to Cooperate on Interactive-Video System Standards," *Wall Street Journal,* April 21, p. B8.

Ziegler, Bart. 1994b. "Layoffs and Overhaul at Unprodigious Prodigy," *Wall Street Journal,* December 6, pp. B1 and B4.

Ziegler, Bart. 1994c. "Mutual Attraction of Phone and Cable Giants Fades Fast," *Wall Street Journal,* April 7, pp. B1 and B8.

Ziegler, Bart, and Mark Robichaux. 1994. "Mutual Attraction of Phone and Cable Giants Fades Fast," *Wall Street Journal,* April 7, pp. B1 and B8.

Appendixes

A

Colloquium Participants

Alden F. Abbott
National Telecommunications and
  Information Administration
U.S. Department of Commerce

John Adam
IEEE Spectrum

Alfred V. Aho
Bell Communications Research

Jonathan D. Aronson
University of Southern California

Jordan Baruch
Jordan Baruch Consulting

Audrey Bashkin
Government Operations Committee
U.S. House of Representatives

Gwen Bell
Association of Computing Machinery

John Blair
Raytheon Research Division

Michael Borrus
Berkeley Roundtable on the
  International Economy

Charles N. Brownstein
National Science Foundation

Daniel F. Burton
Council on Competitiveness

Linda Cashdan
Voice of America

Bill Caswell
Apple Computer Inc.

John S. Cavallini
U.S. Department of Energy

Randall Coleman
Federal Communications Commission

NOTE: Affiliations listed are those current at the time of the colloquium in June 1993.

Peter F. Cowhey
University of California at San Diego

Roger Dannenberg
Carnegie Mellon University

John G. Dardis
U.S. Department of State

Paul David
Stanford University

Gary Demos
DemoGraFX

Marvin Denicoff
Thinking Machines Corporation

Diane DeSimone
Institute for Information Studies
Northern Telecom

Marcia De Sonne
National Association of Broadcasters

Rick Ducey
National Association of Broadcasters

Yona Ettinger
Embassy of Israel

David J. Farber
University of Pennsylvania

Charles Ferguson
Massachusetts Institute of Technology

Charles Firestone
The Aspen Institute

Francis Dummer Fisher
University of Texas at Austin

Michael T.N. Fitch
U.S. Department of State

Thomas Forbord
Office of the Honorable John J.
   Rockefeller IV
U.S. Senate

Laura Ford
US West Inc.

Samuel H. Fuller
Digital Equipment Corporation

Henry Geller
Washington Center for Public Policy
   Research

George Gilder
Discovery Institute

Samuel Ginn
Pacific Telesis Group

Stephen Gould
Congressional Research Service

William Griffin
GTE Laboratories

Edward Heresniak
McGraw-Hill

Anita K. Jones
U.S. Department of Defense

Anne Jones
Sutherland, Asbill, & Brennan

Brian Kahin
Interactive Multimedia Association

Sidney Karin
San Diego Supercomputer Center

Ken Kay
Computer Systems Policy Project

Stephen T. Kent
BBN Communications

David A. Kettler
BellSouth Corporation

Susan Kollins
International Trade Commission

Richard A. Lanham
University of California at Los
    Angeles and Rhetorica Inc.

Alfred M. Lee
National Telecommunications and
    Information Administration
U.S. Department of Commerce

Bruce A. Lehman
U.S. Patent and Trademark Office

Lois Levine-Elman
Biotechnology Law Report

Talbot S. Lindstrom
Federal Trade Commission

Andrew Lippman
Massachusetts Institute of Technology

Robert W. Lucky
Bell Communications Research

William Maher
National Telecommunications and
    Information Administration
U.S. Department of Commerce

Nancy Mason
US West Inc.

Sylvia McDonough
International Trade Commission

Bernadette McGuire
Association of Public TV Stations

John E. McPhee
U.S. Department of Commerce

Steven J. Metalitz
Information Industry Association

Brady Metheny
Washington FAX

David C. Nagel
AppleSoft Inc.

David B. Nelson
U.S. Department of Energy

Michael R. Nelson
Office of Science and Technology
    Policy
Executive Office of the President

Eli M. Noam
Columbia University

Toshiyuki Noguchi
Nomura Research

Donald A. Norman
Apple Computer Inc.

Richard C. Notebaert
Ameritech

Janice Obuchowski
Freedom Technologies Inc.

Eric Pamer
Commerce Clearing House

Ruth S. Raubitschek
U.S. Department of Justice

Howard Rausch
Capital Gains

John J. Reagan
Walt Disney Pictures and Television

Margaret Ryan
Electronic Engineering Times

Gabi Schindler
Apple Computer Inc.

Mary Shaw
Carnegie Mellon University

John F. Shoch
Asset Management Company

Wendy Silberman
Office of the U.S. Trade
   Representative

Alexander Singer
Film Director

James K. Smith
Ameritech

Philip M. Smith
National Research Council

Robert Spinrad
Xerox Corporation

Robert Stein
Voyager Company

Scott Stevens
Carnegie Mellon University

Glenn Strait
The World and I

Steve Tansey
American Chemical Society

Minna Taylor
Fox Broadcasting Company

Michael Telson
Budget Committee
U.S. House of Representatives

Sherry Turkle
Massachusetts Institute of Technology

Andrew J. Viterbi
Qualcomm Inc.

David Walden
BBN Communications

Bill Warlick
International Trade Commission

Steven S. Wildman
Northwestern University

Dale Williams
Sprint Communications

Robert Winter
University of California at Los
   Angeles

William Wulf
University of Virginia

B

Colloquium Agenda

June 8, 1993

7:30 - 8:30 a.m.   **Registration and Continental Breakfast (Lecture Room)**

8:30 - 8:45   **Welcome and Colloquium Introduction**
- William Wulf, *CSTB Chair*
- David Nagel, *Colloquium Chair*

8:45 - 11:00   **Convergence Vision: Beyond Entertainment—and Getting There**
Robert Lucky, Panel Chair
- John Sculley, Apple Computer
- Samuel Ginn, Pacific Telesis
- Robert Stein, Voyager
- Richard Notebaert, Ameritech
- Alexander Singer, Film Director
- Paul David, Stanford University

11:00 - 11:45   **Convergence Realized: A Musical Illustration**
- Robert Winter, University of California at Los Angeles

11:45 - 12:30 p.m.   **Lunch (Refectory)**

12:30 - 2:15   **Economics and Policy: Supply, Demand, and Intervention Issues**
                        Peter Cowhey, Panel Chair
                        • Michael Borrus, Berkeley Roundtable on the International Economy
                        • Peter Cowhey, University of California at San Diego
                        • Eli Noam, Columbia University
                        • Steven Wildman, Northwestern University

2:15 - 2:30   **Break**

2:30 - 4:00   **Techno-pork, Techno-porn, and Techno-pop: Legal and Social Issues**
                        Janice Obuchowski, Panel Chair
                        • George Gilder
                        • Richard Lanham, University of California at Los Angeles
                        • Donald Norman, Apple Computer
                        • Sherry Turkle, Massachusetts Institute of Technology

4:00 - 4:30   **Summary and Concluding Remarks**
                        Colloquium Steering Committee

4:30   **Adjourn**

C

Follow-up Interviews

Stephen M. Case
America Online

Peter F. Cowhey
Federal Communications Commission

Esther Dyson
EDventure Holdings Inc.

Samuel H. Fuller
Digital Equipment Corporation

Robert L. Johnson
Black Entertainment Television

Robert W. Lucky
Bell Communications Research

David C. Nagel
AppleSoft Inc.

Richard C. Notebaert
Ameritech

Janice Obuchowski
Freedom Technologies Inc.

Alexander Singer
Film Director

Robert Stein
Voyager Company

Nancy Stover
YourChoice TV/Discovery Networks
Inc.

Steven S. Wildman
Northwestern University